Not Part of the Bargain:

The Warping of Workers' Compensation

Patricia Hicks

Chapters

CHAPTER 1

I fail to walk safely

One Wednesday morning in December of 2016, I arrived at work just as usual following an uneventful drive. All the roads between home and work had been cleared of the season's first freezing precipitation, which had fallen overnight. I parked, got out of my car, and started walking toward my building. The lot was covered in large patches of snow, which unfortunately wasn't unusual. I work at an Air Force base that doesn't have an easy time clearing its many parking lots and sidewalks in bad weather and tends to be apathetic about even trying. Until that day, I had never had trouble walking through snow, and I didn't realize that much of what looked like snow was actually sheet ice. It was cold outside, so I walked fast.

I made it fewer than ten steps before my right foot found no traction at all and slid out from under me in an instant, landing me on my upper back. I knew I was badly hurt. I knew even before the moment of impact that it was going to be bad. But I did what most people do when they fall in public. I scrambled back to my feet as quickly as I could, despite excruciating pain. There was no one else in sight. Crossing 40 more yards of icy parking lot to reach my building was unthinkable. It was all I could do to hobble back to my car and get back in and call my husband, who sent my supervisor a quick email telling him what had happened. Just wanting to get home as soon as possible, I drove myself there (foolishly, because I couldn't turn my head). An x-ray and MRI later showed that

I had crushed two vertebrae; one by about 40% and the other by about 10% of its original height.

I took only a week off work, pushing myself to return as soon as possible because I so wanted my normal life back. I had never been seriously injured before—maybe that's why I was unrealistically hopeful that this accident was something I'd be able to put behind me quickly. Back at work, I was still in significant pain, which worsened as the day wore on. By midafternoon each day, I couldn't find a comfortable position in my desk chair. My primary doctor referred me to a neurosurgeon, who then referred me to another with more experience treating injuries high in the spine. The second neurosurgeon recommended an operation that was approved within days by my group health insurer and went a mercifully long way toward relieving my pain.

One advantage (or disadvantage, depending on your perspective) to being an engineer is that during the week I was off work, I was able to keep up with my job from home, using a laptop. The day after the accident, my supervisor emailed me a form called OWCP-915 *Claim for Medical Reimbursement*. Instructions printed on the back explained, "This form is to be used to seek reimbursement for out of pocket medical expenses pertaining to the treatment of an accepted condition." So apparently, I had to get my condition "accepted" somehow and then I could recoup my medical copays. It would never have occurred to me to ask my employing agency to pay any part of my medical bills, but when I saw that they were offering, I thought, why not? That seemed only fair, under the circumstances.

I had already electronically submitted an Occupational Safety and Health Administration Form 301 (OSHA-301) per my supervisor's direction. The OSHA-301 is just an injury and illness incident report and does not establish a claim for workers' compensation, though for federal civilian employees it is a prerequisite for filing a claim. My OSHA-301 submittal prompted a phone call I received the following week from a young-sounding safety officer. I was in my office and not too happy about being asked to describe my ungraceful fall within earshot of a dozen or so coworkers, but I obliged. After listening to my account of slipping on sheet ice in our parking lot and breaking my back, the officer advised me that I could prevent such accidents in the future by walking like a duck, toes turned outward.

In a similarly helpful vein, my building manager sent the following email out to all the building's inhabitants the day after my injury:

> All,
>
> If need be, please divert your normal route to avoid walking on known slick spots. Many of you walk through the drive to get to door six. [Civil Engineering] has yet to salt the parking lots, so this area is still very slick. Please use the main sidewalk to avoid possible injuries. Hopefully the lots will be salted soon.

Unpersuaded that walking like a duck and avoiding "known slick spots" would be enough to save me from another fall, which I feared might be devastating if it happened before I had fully healed, I asked my doctor for a handicapped parking permit. It turned out to be a mild winter, but one day following a light storm, I was grateful to have a prime parking spot. I picked my way carefully to the door of my building, like a very slow duck with a broken back. The sidewalk that ran along the handicapped row was covered with ice.

Here are some things I thought I knew about workers' compensation going into it. Maybe you think you know them, too:

1. Workers' compensation is a gift from employers to their employees.
2. Workers' compensation benefits are generous.
3. It's common for employees to fake or exaggerate injuries in order to collect workers' compensation.

CHAPTER 2

The myth that workers' compensation is a gift from employers to employees

On November 15, 1902, Charlestown Navy Yard employee Gustavus A. Smith inadvertently stepped backward knee-deep into a barrel of scalding water fed by a steam exhaust pipe. The barrel was sunk level with the ground and had no guard around it. Some doctors later told him his leg was "parbroiled" and should have been amputated, but one Dr. Andrews applied salves to "eat off all the dead flesh down to the bone to save it." Mr. Smith was confined to his bed for six months, suffering what he later described as torture, before he was able to return to the navy yard with the aid of a cane. He wasn't as productive he had been before the accident, and so he dealt with wage reduction and frequent layoffs.[1]

On October 13, 1905, John Fletcher, an employee of the Boston Navy Yard steam engineering department, was mangled by an electric crane he happened to be standing near when an inattentive coworker turned it on. John's left hand was crushed and made permanently deformed and all but useless, his right arm was cut off at the shoulder, a cut on his head required stitches, and the ribs on the right side of his body were torn from his backbone. It was six months before he was able to perform any sort of manual labor again, and even years later he was unable to dress himself or, as he delicately phrased it in a statement submitted to Congress, "attend to the necessities of nature."[2]

The Boston Navy Yard recorded a total of 82 civilian injuries between 1902 and 1907 in the steam engineering department alone.

Severely cut or crushed hands and crushed feet were common af-flictions, but plenty of others were recorded as well. A few entries stand out:

> October 1, 1904. Hubert Sulkey, iron finisher's helper, struck by flying piece of iron while breaking same for foundry use. He died a few hours after, never having regained his senses. Left a wife and five small children destitute.

> December 8, 1904. James Miller, boilermaker helper, badly injured all over.

> September 19, 1906. Walter Burke, boy boiler scaler, se-vere injury to testicles, being struck with a large spike.[3]

Rapid industrialization in the late 1800s and early 1900s created a crisis of occupational injuries, diseases, and deaths that the United States was ill-equipped to handle. There was no national welfare system at the time. States, local governments, and private charities typically assumed voluntary responsibility for taking care of the poor. Cash might be provided to the most "deserving" among them—widows and their young children, the elderly, and the to-tally disabled. For the rest, orphanages and poorhouses were dreaded last resorts. The elderly commonly sank into poverty upon losing their employability. It can be difficult for Americans today to fully appreciate how precarious life was in the era before Presi-dent Franklin D. Roosevelt enacted Social Security in 1935, provid-ing retirement pensions, unemployment insurance, and cash assis-tance to the impoverished and the disabled. In 1908, George Cain, then President of the National League of Government Employees, testified before Congress that "with the average man who works for a living, hunger or starvation is only a matter of two weeks away from him when he is out of work, or when his wages cease."[4] Mr. Cain was arguing in favor of implementing a workers' com-pensation system.

Workers' compensation was innovated by German Chancellor Otto von Bismark, whose 1884 Accident Bill was rapidly adopted in various forms by most of Europe before reaching North America. Prior to the enactment of workers' compensation laws, an injured worker in the U.S. could file a lawsuit charging his or her employer with negligence, which is a type of "tort" or civil wrongdoing, as opposed to a crime. Employers defended themselves in court using three common law defenses known as the "unholy trinity": the *assumption of risk* defense applied if the injury had resulted from an ordinary hazard of employment of which the worker should have been aware; the *fellow worker rule* defense applied if the injury had been caused by a coworker's negligence; and the *contributory negligence* defense applied if the worker's own negligence had contributed to the injury in any way, to any extent at all.

With these expansive defenses at their disposal, employers prevailed in court a majority of the time. However, they paid lawyer, court, and witness fees regardless, and they antagonized labor and the general public by profiting from risky industries while being affected little by the dead and disabled bodies left in their wake. In 1913, the rate of industrial fatalities was 61 out of every 100,000 workers—more than seventeen times the incidence today.[5] Some injured workers received compensation voluntarily provided by their employers, or from sickness and accident funds into which they had paid dues, but many received no compensation at all and became dependent on charity, or left family members dependent on charity if they died.

The prospect of suing one's employer was daunting, and the process wasteful. It might take years to have a case tried in backlogged courts, while the injured worker went without income. Premiums paid by employers who purchased liability insurance went mostly toward operating costs and profits for insurers, court costs, and witness and attorney fees. After accounting for those expenses and the portion of any award owed the injured workers' attorney, no more than 25% of the money paid into the tort system by employers reached injured workers or their dependents.[6] There was growing public pressure for laws that would force employers to share more evenly and efficiently in the risks of their trades.

Various states enacted Employer Liability laws, which weakened or eliminated some of the employers' common-law defenses. These proved largely ineffective though, because the onus remained on injured workers to show appreciable negligence on the part of their employers. The reason that was hard to do was explained by an article published in the March 1912 edition of the Michigan Law Review. The article presented an analysis of data on industrial accidents in various states and in Germany, concluding that 44% of them could not have been prevented through the exercise of reasonable due care because they were due to "acts of God" or were "inevitable accidents connected with the employment." The avoidable 56% of accidents included 29% for which the injured worker alone was blamed, 5% for which the employer and employee shared blame, and 5% for which a fellow worker was blamed. Only 17% of industrial accidents were attributed solely to the negligence or fault of the employer; this value, 17%, represented the theoretical maximum proportion of cases in which an injured worker could hope for full recovery under the tort system. In practice, the percentage awarded any compensation at all in court was closer to half that amount.[7]

Even a win for the injured worker could be an underwhelming victory; court awards were typically quite a bit lower (even accounting for inflation) than the multimillion-dollar judgments familiar to us today. In Ohio in the year 1911, court awards and settlements secured by families of fatally injured workers averaged $949, with few exceeding $5,000. After paying attorney fees of 25% and another $200 or so for funeral expenses, the average family was left with about $500; at the time, $600 (equivalent to about $16,500 in 2020) was considered the minimum annual income needed to support a family of five. The workers' compensation law Ohio enacted in 1911 was comparatively generous, guaranteeing $2,400 to the survivors of a workman who had been earning $600 per year when he died, with no court proceedings required.[8]

Workers' compensation was a deal agreed upon by business and labor leaders whereby employers compensate workers on a no-fault basis for their injuries in return for limits that are lower than what might have been awarded in court. The compensation is intended to replace a portion of the worker's financial losses in connection with his or her injury, with no consideration for intangible human costs such as pain and suffering, and no punitive fines. This deal was hailed as the "Grand Bargain," and where it exists, it is almost always the exclusive remedy for occupational injuries and diseases. Employees do not have the option of suing their employers instead of accepting benefits unless the harm inflicted on them was intentional. For their part, employers must compensate any work-related injury that doesn't stem from willful misconduct, an intent to self-injure, or intoxication by alcohol or illegal drugs.

President Theodore Roosevelt was a strong proponent of workers' compensation. In a message to Congress on January 31, 1908, he called it "a matter of humiliation to the nation that there should not be on our statute books provision to meet and partially to atone for cruel misfortune when it comes upon a man, through no fault of his own, while faithfully serving the public."[9] Four months later, on May 30, 1908, Congress passed a workers' compensation law that covered about a fourth of federal civilian employees—those with especially hazardous jobs in manufacturing establishments, arsenals, navy yards, and untamed outdoors. Prior to then, federal employees had been in a more hopeless position than most to obtain redress for workplace injuries because the government enjoys sovereign immunity, meaning it cannot be sued by its own citizens. But with passage of the 1908 act, federal employees gained the advantage, because only they were covered by it. The Constitution forbids Congress from meddling with state laws (such as those allowing tort suits and common law defenses) except to govern interstate commerce, and until 1937, the U.S. Supreme Court narrowly interpreted interstate commerce to exclude manufacturing. Therefore, state manufacturing-related issues such as injuries were considered beyond the reach of federal lawmakers.

On May 3, 1911, Wisconsin implemented the first state workers' compensation law that would survive court challenges. New York's first attempt, a law enacted in 1910, was ruled unconstitutional by the New York Supreme Court on the grounds that penalizing employers without regard to fault amounted to taking property from them without the due process guaranteed by the Fourteenth Amendment.[10] The very next day, March 25, 1911, 146 garment workers died in the Triangle Shirtwaist Factory fire. The victims, ranging in age from 14 to 46, worked 52 hours a week and were unable to escape the burning building—except by jumping to their deaths—because the doors were locked to prevent unauthorized breaks or theft. New York responded by crafting a constitutional amendment to accommodate its workers' compensation law, which was then reenacted with minor changes in 1913.

Most of the early adopting states, New York included, had workers' compensation laws that applied only to hazardous industries and covered only accidents, not occupational diseases. Medical aid, if provided at all, was limited to a narrow post-injury timeframe and dollar amount. Wisconsin's 1911 law was the first with broad applicability and coverage, but it was elective for employers, who were deprived of the common law defenses if they chose not to participate. New York's law was compulsory, and after its halting progress through the state Supreme Court, many doubted it could withstand a similar challenge at the federal level. However, in March 1917, the U.S. Supreme Court erased those doubts by upholding the constitutionality of both mandatory and elective state workers' compensation laws.[11] Most states soon enacted laws of their own, and by 1949 every state had a workers' compensation program of one kind or another.

In the late 1930s, the U.S. Supreme Court's interpretation of the Commerce Clause relaxed so that a uniform nationwide workers' compensation law could have been enacted by the federal government. By then, though, most states had programs of their own, over which they were resistant to giving up control. Efforts to develop a single overarching federal program are still initiated from time to time but are invariably obstructed by holders of state administrative powers that grow increasingly ingrained with time.[12] This is unfortunate, because our nation's piecemeal approach to defining workers' compensation benefits has rested the physical and financial security of its workers on quicksand, doomed to being sunk ever lower by state legislatures competing to attract businesses. It's a problem that was recognized from the very start. On March 23, 1908, Commissioner of Labor Charles Neill addressed the following observation to Congressmen who were deciding details of the first federal employees' compensation act: "In the domain left outside of Congressional action the United States will necessarily be behind the civilized world in all its relations of this kind. No state wants to put a burden upon itself, upon its industries, that is not borne by the industries of another State…"[13]

Hon. Charles Reid (D-AR) then raised another interesting point by asking, "Is the burden upon the industry; is it not upon the consumer?" Mr. Neill answered, "Primarily it is placed on the industry, and then on the consumer." On the surface, it might seem that employers alone bear the cost of workers' compensation benefits, since they pay the bill for insurance premiums (or directly for benefits if self-insured). But of course, employers must balance those outlays, along with wages paid to workers and every other operating expense, against income drivers such as sales volumes and prices charged to consumers, so as to ensure themselves a worthwhile profit. Purchasing insurance to cover claims makes the overall burden predictable and easier to pass on to others. In effect, it is impossible to gauge exactly how costs are ultimately apportioned among employers, employees, and consumers. There are even three states—New Mexico, Oregon, and Washington—in which employees are required to make regular payroll contributions to help offset the cost of workers' compensation benefits.[14]

In most states, workers' compensation insurance can be purchased from a private insurer, with or without a deductible. Twenty-one states operate their own workers' compensation insurance funds, which either compete with private insurers or are the exclusive source of coverage for employers. Premiums charged by state fund managers or private insurers usually depend on an employer's particular risk as assessed in two ways: by category of work (e.g., construction is riskier than office work) and, for large employers, an experience rating that takes their claim histories into account. Employers with sufficient capital generally may self-insure after receiving permission from their state. In 2018, 55.3% of all workers' comp benefits were paid by private insurers, 14.1% were paid by state funds, and 25.1% were paid by self-insured employers. The remaining 5.5% were paid by the federal government.[15] Civilian employees of all federal government agencies located throughout the U.S. are covered by a workers' compensation system administered by the Department of Labor. That system, which also extends to private sector employees in a few very hazardous jobs, is described in the next chapter.

CHAPTER 3

The FECA

On September 7, 1916, a new Federal Employees' Compensation Act (FECA) superseded the 1908 statute, which was by then widely regarded as deficient. Dr. I.M. Rubinow, an insurance company statistician who collaborated on both acts, later apologized for the groundbreaking one, saying, "In 1908 we passed this compensation law, and we were rather timid about such legislation, and we passed a compensation scale that was utterly inadequate, but which at that time seemed too high."[16] The 1908 act covered only employees in especially hazardous jobs, and only those who suffered accidental injuries, not occupational diseases; it provided full wage replacement for up to one year if disability persisted that long, and a second year at half wages for postal workers only. It did not pay for medical treatment, and wage replacement benefits were not payable if the injury was caused by the worker's own negligence. The 1916 act rectified all those shortcomings; it covered virtually all federal employees for both occupational injuries and diseases, provided wage replacement for the entire duration of disability, and paid for medical treatment. Some degree of negligence on the part of the worker was no longer a barrier to receiving benefits, though of course willful misconduct did (and still does) disqualify a claim.

The FECA is codified in Title 5, Chapter 81 of the U.S. Code. Its two most overarching sections, 8102 and 8103, are copied below.

5 U.S.C. 8102. Compensation for disability or death of employee

(a) The United States shall pay compensation as specified by this subchapter for the disability or death of an employee resulting from personal injury sustained while in the performance of his duty, unless the injury or death is—

1. caused by willful misconduct of the employee;
2. caused by the employee's intention to bring about the injury or death of himself or of another; or
3. caused by the intoxication of the injured employee.

5 U.S.C. 8103. Medical services and initial medical and other benefits

(a) The United States shall furnish to an employee who is injured while in the performance of duty, the services, appliances, and supplies prescribed or recommended by a qualified physician, which the Secretary of Labor considers likely to cure, give relief, reduce the degree or the period of disability, or aid in lessening the amount of the monthly compensation. These services, appliances, and supplies shall be furnished—

1. whether or not disability has arisen;
2. notwithstanding that the employee has accepted or is entitled to receive benefits under subchapter III of chapter 83 of this title or another retirement system for employees of the Government; and
3. by or on the order of United States medical officers and hospitals, or, at the employee's option, by or on the order of physicians and hospitals designated or approved by the Secretary.

The Code of Federal Regulations (CFR) contains all the rules and regulations ("administrative law") published by agencies of the U.S. Federal Government. Rules governing administration of the FECA are laid out in CFR Title 20, Part 10, "Claims for

Compensation under the Federal Employees' Compensation Act, as Amended." The introductory section 10.0 is copied below:

20 CFR 10.0 What are the provisions of the FECA, in general?

The Federal Employees' Compensation Act (FECA) as amended (5 U.S.C. 8101 et seq.) provides for the payment of workers' compensation benefits to civilian officers and employees of all branches of the Government of the United States. The regulations in this part describe the rules for filing, processing, and paying claims for benefits under the FECA. Proceedings under the FECA are non-adversarial in nature.

FECA administration is the responsibility of the Secretary of Labor, who delegates it to the Office of Workers' Compensation Programs (OWCP). The OWCP has four divisions, each of which administers a separate disability compensation program. The Division of Federal Employees' Compensation (DFEC) is the one that administers the FECA. The DFEC has a national office in Washington, D.C. and 12 district offices situated to cover every region of the United States. The other three divisions of OWCP administer compensation governed not by the FECA but by three other distinct acts for: (1) individuals made ill by exposure to radiation as a result of nuclear weapons testing or uranium mining; (2) maritime workers who are injured while working over navigable waters; and (3) coal miners with black lung disease.

To claim FECA benefits, a federal employee who sustains a work-related traumatic injury must give notice of it on Form CA-1, and an employee who has a disease which he or she believes to be work-related must give notice of it on Form CA-2, within three years of the injury or onset of the disease, but preferably within 30 days. Exceptions are made to the three-year filing deadline if the employer gained knowledge of the injury or disease within 30 days in some other manner. In cases of latent disability, the time for filing a claim does not begin to run until the employee becomes aware, or reasonably should have been aware, of the causal relationship between the disability and the employment.

Detailed information about the FECA is published by the Department of Labor in "Injury Compensation for Federal Employees," Publication CA-810.[17] The front page of CA-810 states that it is "meant to serve as a handbook for Federal agency personnel specialists, compensation specialists, and supervisors." I will add that it's also a useful resource for injured workers. In brief, the FECA provides six types of benefits for federal employees who sustain injuries or diseases in performance of their duties. These are:

1. 100% of injury-related medical costs;

2. up to 45 calendar days of leave for recovery after a traumatic injury;

3. partial replacement of lost wages if disability continues beyond 45 days;

4. monetary compensation for loss of, or lost function of, certain body parts;

5. vocational rehabilitation services; and

6. a prescribed amount for funeral and burial expenses, as well as monetary compensation to survivors of an employee whose death resulted from a work-related condition.

Funds are appropriated from Congress to cover OWCP's administrative expenses and to maintain a sufficient reserve for payment of benefits. Once a year, the Secretary of Labor furnishes a statement to each employing agency of payments made from the Employees' Compensation Fund on account of injuries sustained or diseases contracted by its employees, and those costs must be reimbursed by the employing agency. This chargeback process was instituted in 1960 with the intent of promoting safety by increasing accountability.[18] But agencies include FECA costs in their annual budget requests to Congress, so in practice, money just takes a detour through the various agencies on its way from Congress to the Compensation Fund. The U.S. Postal Service, which operates off revenues rather than taxpayer money, has to reimburse OWCP for its share of administrative costs as well as for benefits.

An injured worker who disputes any decision made by OWCP has three avenues of appeal: (1) a formal written request for reconsideration by the OWCP district office; (2) an oral hearing or review of the written record before an OWCP representative; or (3) a hearing before the Employees' Compensation Appeals Board (ECAB). FECA administration differs from state workers' compensation programs in that there is no involvement of the courts. Whereas decisions of state administrators can be appealed all the way up to the state Supreme Court and potentially even to the U.S. Supreme Court, the ECAB is the highest and final authority in FECA appeals. There are three ECAB members, all of whom are appointed by the Secretary of Labor. They are authorized to review questions of law, fact, and exercise of discretion, considering only evidence that was in the employee's case record when OWCP made the decision being appealed. The ECAB is touted as being completely independent of OWCP, though the Secretary of Labor oversees and directs the OWCP and also appoints the ECAB judges and decides their rules and regulations. The Frances Perkins building in Washington, D.C. cozily houses the Secretary of Labor, the ECAB judges, and OWCP's National Office.

CHAPTER 4

OHIO

Ohio BWC

I live in Ohio, which is the most populous of only four states (the others are North Dakota, Washington, and Wyoming) that have an *exclusive* state workers' compensation fund. Exclusive state-managed funds are, by definition, the sole source of workers' compensation insurance for employers operating in that state; all must pay into the fund except federal employing agencies and private employers who obtain permission to self-insure. There are another 17 states with *non-exclusive* funds that compete with private insurers. South Carolina's fund is exclusive for state and local government employers but competes for the rest of the market. In 28 states and the District of Columbia, employers must buy a policy from a private insurer unless approved to self-insure.[19]

Like all other states either with or without state funds, Ohio vests administrative responsibility for its workers' compensation program in a special state agency—in this case, the Ohio Bureau of Workers' Compensation (BWC). I examine BWC frequently throughout this book, mostly for a sense check to help identify which of my experiences with OWCP reflect features that are common to workers' compensation programs in general. Ohio BWC is led by an administrator who employs, directs, and supervises other bureau employees, determines premium rates for businesses, and sets rules and standards for the handling of claims. Ohio law authorizes the governor to appoint the BWC Administrator, stipulating that "a person appointed to the position of Administrator shall possess significant management experience in effectively managing an organization or organizations of substantial size and complexity" and that "the governor shall not appoint any person who has, or whose spouse has, given a contribution to the campaign committee of the governor in an amount greater than one thousand dollars during the two-year period immediately preceding the date of the appointment of the administrator."[20]

Ohio BWC has a board of directors made up of 11 members appointed by the governor with the advice and consent of the Senate. Serving on the Board is not a full-time job, but at minimum it convenes twelve times a year. The Board approves administrative and investment policies for the Bureau, arranges and reviews independent financial counsel and audits, and studies issues put forward by the administrator or governor. It also submits an annual report evaluating BWC's performance against cost and quality objectives. Board members are required by law to represent diverse perspectives and skills as reflected in their vocations and affiliations, with one member representing employees, two representing employee organizations, three representing employers, and one representing the public; there must also be two investment and securities experts, one certified public accountant, and one actuary. The governor selects a Board chairperson from among its members to lead.[21]

Every private employer in Ohio is required by law to submit a payroll report to BWC annually, detailing the number of employees it has, their wages, and the types of work they perform. BWC uses this information to calculate an appropriate annual premium rate for the employer. Those that demonstrate sufficient financial strength and administrative ability are allowed to self-insure. Self-insuring employers don't pay full premiums but must contribute to a self-insuring employers' guaranty fund that is used to pay any benefits the employer can't. A self-insured employer has the authority to accept or reject claims for benefits and to approve payment of benefits, subject to the rules and regulations of the Bureau.

The employer must contract with health care providers and ensure medical services are obtainable during all working hours at least. Special procedures must be established for the resolution of medical disputes.[22]

BWC has what it calls a Health Partnership Program (HPP) for managing medical care. Ohio employers that aren't self-insured must choose a Managed Care Organization (MCO) from a list of 12 currently on contract with BWC. The MCO manages the medical portion of claims, which entails approving medical treatments, processing medical bills, making provider payments, and helping employers establish return-to-work programs. When an Ohio employee is injured at work, the employee and initial treating physician fill out a First Report of an Injury, Occupational Disease, or Death (FROI) form, which is routed to BWC. BWC decides whether the injury is compensable, and if it is, disburses cash benefit payments directly to the employee and medical benefit payments to the MCO to be further disbursed to providers.[23] Any surplus premiums collected from Ohio businesses are invested. When surpluses are larger than necessary to safeguard solvency of the fund, BWC may reduce premiums or even issue partial refunds to employers.[24]

If an injured worker or his employer disagrees with a BWC decision to accept or reject a claim, either of them may appeal to the Ohio Industrial Commission, which hears appeals at three levels: first at the district hearing officer level, then at the staff hearing officer level, and finally, at the Commission level. The hearing officers at the district and staff levels are all attorneys. Commission level appeals are heard by a panel of three members appointed by the governor and confirmed by Ohio's Senate. By previous employment, vocation, or affiliation, one member must represent employers, another must represent employees, and the third must represent the public. After exhausting all three Industrial Commission appeal levels, either party may bring further action before a County Court of Common Pleas. Decisions regarding denial of medical treatment are appealed first through an alternative dispute resolution process and then through the process outlined above.[25]

The Ohio legislature created an ombudsperson system in the 1970s to help employers and employees navigate the workers' compensation system. The BWC Administrator is required by law to provide office space, supplies, and clerical assistance for the ombuds program, which is funded out of BWC's budget. The Ombuds Office is designed to be a neutral and independent body which answers questions, investigates complaints, and mediates wherever possible to resolve problems with BWC or the Industrial Commission. The ombuds staff also analyzes inquiry and complaint data and publishes an annual report highlighting areas most in need of improvement.[26]

CHAPTER 5

Can I get a little help here?

When I decided to file for workers' compensation, I had trouble locating and then editing the required claim form CA-1 on the Federal Employees' Compensation Operations & Management Portal (ECOMP), so I sought help. The ECOMP website didn't list a phone number, but there was an option to request help via email. I did that and got an automatically generated response that provided a contact email for further assistance; but it was the same one I had just used. I tried it anyway, and sure enough, my email bounced right back to me again with a suggestion that I send my question to the same place. I called my base's Personnel Office but was told they know nothing about workers' compensation and I ought to call my division's Human Resources group. I called Human Resources but was told they know nothing about it either and I ought to call my building's Safety Manager. I called my Safety Manager, who told me he knows nothing about it and suggested I call the base's Occupational Medicine Clinic. I called the clinic and was told they only help military personnel, not civilians like myself. I waited a day, then repeated the whole round of calls, hoping the phones had just been answered by the wrong people the first time. But my second round of calls went exactly the same. I started calling numbers I found online that seemed promising, but those all led to conversations with people who had no idea what I was talking about, or who gave me bad guidance, or who forwarded me on to someone else who couldn't help me either.

It was becoming apparent that my agency was not at all interested in helping me file a workers' comp claim, and I guess I can't blame them. But it's not directly in my employer's best interest to help me sign up for subsidized health insurance, either, or to help retirees claim their pensions, yet they do help with those things. My employing agency even sponsors free classes on Social Security benefits, which cost the agency more money than workers' compensation. In the U.S., the most expensive employee benefit is subsidized health insurance, which in 2019 accounted for 8.3% of total civilian payroll and 7.9% of private industry payroll. Employer contributions to Social Security and Medicare comprised another 5.6% of payroll for civilian workers and 5.9% for those in private industry. Workers' compensation costs represented 1.3% of total payroll in both categories, looming large only in comparison to the 0.5% combined federal and state taxes for unemployment insurance.[27] Relative to most other benefits, workers' compensation isn't particularly expensive, but there are other qualities that make it the pariah of job-related benefits:

1. Health insurance and retirement benefits are bargaining chips for attracting and keeping employees. There is a payoff for making those programs competitive and well-managed. In contrast, I'm pretty sure no one has ever asked in a job interview about the prospective employer's worker's compensation program.

2. Most employees take advantage of employer-subsidized health insurance and retirement benefits. There would be an outcry if those programs failed to live up to their promise. In contrast, only a small percentage ever file for workers' compensation.

3. Employers are taxed a fixed percentage of payroll for Social Security and Medicare, regardless of how many of their employees use – or ever will use – those benefits. State unemployment insurance taxes have an experience-based component that drives up cost for employers who engender a high number of claims, but that's a hit employers weigh and ultimately choose for themselves when laying off or letting go good employees to achieve overall savings. With workers' compensation, employers can

take a hit for every claim filed, either in the form of direct payments or higher premiums, but with no choice in the matter and nothing in it for them. This makes filing a claim personal, and adversarial by default.

There is a Department of Defense Instruction (DoDI 1400.25-V810) that defines how injury compensation is supposed to be implemented within the Department, outlining responsibilities of all the players involved. Civilian Personnel is charged with "providing operational guidance, advice, and assistance concerning injury compensation matters." Each Civilian Personnel or Human Resources Office is instructed to "designate a staff member as Injury Compensation Program Administrator (ICPA) to oversee the program, to coordinate the efforts of all involved management officials, and to ensure optimum effectiveness in program administration." The ICPA is assigned numerous specific duties, but "one of the primary functions of the ICPA is to provide counsel and assistance to injured employees as well as to supervisors."[28]

If such a thing as an ICPA exists at my base, I didn't turn over the right rock to find it, but I discovered that there is a centralized Injury Compensation Office at Joint Base San Antonio in Randolph, TX. I called their number, thinking surely this must be where I would find answers, at last. The woman who picked up the phone wanted to know first of all if I was an employer or an employee. I told her I was an employee and needed help filing a claim. She took my social security number, then gave me a ticket number and said someone would call me back. When that hadn't happened by the end of the day, I called again. This time I asked what happens when employers call. It turns out, they are put right through to a benefits counselor. How nice that must be. I was given another ticket number and told to expect a call back in the next 24 to 48 hours.

The next day, I got a call from an Injury Compensation Counselor. For the first time in the two months that had elapsed since my accident, I was finally speaking with someone who knew all about workers' compensation. I felt tremendously relieved to finally have a source of guidance; and yet, it was like talking to an opponent's attorney. Her salary was being paid not by me but by the government whose money I was trying to claim, and it showed. Though she was polite, she sounded defensive and volunteered no information whatsoever, giving only short, direct answers to the questions I knew to ask. At one point, she chided me for not just following the guidance posted on my break room wall. I told her I'm an engineer and don't have a break room wall, and no doubt that was part of my problem—it stands to reason that people with more physical jobs would be more likely to have coworkers and supervisors who have experience with workers' compensation and can help them.

Lack of guidance can cost employees dearly. FECA includes a benefit called "Continuation of Pay (COP)," which consists of paid time off as needed within the first 45 days post-injury to recuperate and attend medical appointments. I nearly lost out on it because I didn't file Form CA-1 within 30 days of my injury, which is a prerequisite for receiving COP. In the ECOMP web portal, there was a link labeled "File new form" and a radio button labeled "File new OSHA-301, CA-1, or CA-2." Following those seemingly obvious paths only led me to the option of filing another OSHA-301 form. Meanwhile, the status of the OSHA-301 I had already submitted was stalled at "Pending final review by OSHA record keeper." I hadn't yet found anyone I could ask, so I went with my best guess, which was that I must not be able to submit Form CA-1 yet because my OSHA-301 still hadn't been processed. I kept an eye on it and waited. But the status message never changed, and by the time I realized it never would and found the CA-1 link I needed in an obscure drop-down menu beneath the frozen banner, my accident was 64 days behind me.

Missing the 30-day deadline didn't disqualify me from filing a claim, but it could have made me ineligible to keep the COP wages I'd been paid during the week I stayed home and the medical appointments I attended during work hours afterward. An employing agency that objects to providing COP for one of its employees can send a "controversion" letter to that effect to OWCP, though OWCP makes the final decision. I was sincerely grateful for the fact that the time I had to take off work for recovery wasn't charged to my sick or annual leave. I conscientiously kept up with all my job responsibilities, working from home on weekends as needed.

Once my claim was filed, OWCP materialized, first contacting my supervisor with questions he told me were all along the lines of whether or not I steal office supplies. (No, I don't.) Then I received a copy of a letter sent to OWCP by my employing agency, declaring its intention to controvert my COP because of my late submittal of Form CA-1. This meant I would have to give back all the salary I had received during the week I took off work following my injury (even though I had worked from home). I didn't know the man who signed that letter, and I'm sure he didn't know me. It was nothing personal; he was just doing his job. I had missed a deadline, giving my agency an opportunity to save themselves money by controverting my COP, and they were jumping on it. Still, from my perspective at that difficult time, the letter arrived like a sucker punch. Fortunately, OWCP later overturned my agency's controversion; what saved me was the email my husband sent my supervisor minutes after I was injured, which substituted for notice within 30 days on Form CA-1.

Oddly, the COP hours recorded on my Leave and Earnings (L&E) statement never matched the ones I claimed in a given pay period, and in fact the total on my L&E statement froze when it reached 6 hours, far short of the 34 hours I actually used within the allotted timeframe (the day of injury isn't counted as COP). I wasn't personally affected by that discrepancy, because the unacknowledged COP hours were paid as if I had been at work, but I still can't help wondering who out there behind the workers' compensation curtain might have had a vested interest in reporting that my injury was so minor it kept me off work for less than a day.

CHAPTER 6

Should I get a lawyer?
Can I get a lawyer?

The FECA is intended to be remedial in nature, and proceedings under it are non-adversarial.

-Injury Compensation for Federal Employees, Publication CA-810

Workers' compensation is touted as being non-adversarial, meaning that employers and employees are supposed to go into the process with full understanding and agreement regarding which conditions are covered and how benefits are determined. Maybe it really does feel non-adversarial to those who administer the system, who know it inside and out and have nothing to lose from a fumble but kudos at appraisal time. Personally, I felt like I had suddenly been thrust into a game I had only vaguely heard of before, pitted against an invisible team of people who made all the rules and wouldn't fully explain them to me up-front. What I had at stake was thousands of dollars in lost wages and access to medical care.

Nationwide, five to ten percent of workers' compensation claimants hire an attorney, though the proportion of seriously injured workers who do so is one third.[29] Even claimants who don't plan a formal appeal sometimes turn to lawyers for help navigating a system they find frustrating, bewildering, or even hostile. There came a point for me, when my claim was still in limbo and the online searches I resorted to for guidance were turning up horror stories about workers' compensation, when I became so unsure of what I was walking into that I went looking for a lawyer. I wasn't after a settlement; I knew that was out of the question for a federal workers' comp claim involving a back injury. I just wanted someone to sell me an hour's worth of objective information and ungrudging guidance I couldn't find anywhere for free. I called around and found no one in my area willing to take on a federal workers' comp case. One lawyer described OWCP to me as a "mess with inconsistent rules." I gave up on the idea of consulting a lawyer and started hoping my claim would be rejected. I considered withdrawing it but was afraid that might imply it was fraudulent.

I was surprised to learn that workers' compensation administrators, OWCP included, get away with exercising quite a bit of control over a claimant's access to legal representation. OWCP allows claimants to appoint one representative at a time. This must be done in writing, and the representative named will have access to the claimant's file to the same extent as the claimant. Federal employees are not allowed to represent one another, with the exception of immediate family members or while acting in the capacity of union representative. Oddly enough, though a FECA claimant is solely responsible for paying his or her own attorney, win or lose, he or she may not do so until the fee has been approved by OWCP or the Appeals Board. To obtain this approval, the representative must submit a fee application containing an itemized statement of charges, accompanied by a statement signed by the claimant expressing agreement.[30] The existence and long-term survival of such a patronizing rule is a testament to how successful workers' comp administrators have been at selling an image of themselves as devoted protectors of sick and injured workers. It's a strange predicament to find oneself in—unable to hire an attorney to help challenge an organization unless that organization approves the attorney's fee! Most state administrators exercise authority over claimant attorney fees in one way or another, ranging from a cursory review for "reasonableness" to enforcement of oppressively low limits, but it wasn't always this way for FECA claimants.

On April 3, 1914, the House of Representatives convened a hearing on Bill H.R. 15222, known as the McGillicuddy Bill in honor of its sponsor, Congressman Daniel McGillicuddy (D-ME). H.R. 15222 was a draft version of H.R. 15316, the bill that was destined to be approved by Congress and become FECA law in 1916. In the April 1914 hearing, the wording of H.R. 15222 was reviewed section by section. Upon reaching Section 29, which mandated that "no claim for legal services in connection with any claim arising under this act shall be enforceable unless approved by the commission," Congressman Henry Danforth (R-NY) asked, "Against whom would a claim for legal services be enforced, if it were enforced?" Dr. John Beaman answered, "It would be enforced against the claimant. There is no provision in the act for paying lawyers' fees out of the fund. This is simply to protect the employee against the iniquitous lawyer who tries to get all of his money."[31]

Hon. Joseph Taggart (D-KA) interjected to correct Mr. Danforth, explaining that the Section 29 rule was related to Section 30, which applied when a claimant sued a third party (i.e., a person or entity other than his employer who might be liable for causing or contributing to his injury). Section 30 stipulated that after court costs and a "reasonable attorney fee" were paid, the net award must be applied to repaying the Compensation Fund for benefits already received by the employee. Any money left over was his to keep, but would be credited toward future benefit payments—meaning that no more benefits (either wage replacement or medical bill payment) would be available to the injured employee unless and until the cumulative value of benefits he would otherwise have received exceeded the amount of court award he pocketed.[32] This is still true today.[33]

Mr. McGillicuddy was present at the April 1914 hearing, and when this subject came up, he warned his colleagues that a claimant who sues a third party might collude with his lawyer to inflate the lawyer's fee, thereby keeping more money out of the government's reach for them to share. He said, "If you leave it to this commission, so far as the United States is concerned, they are protected. He cannot determine what shall be a reasonable fee; the Government's commission determines that."[34] Far from worrying that naive claimants might be taken advantage of by shrewd lawyers as is commonly presumed, the sponsor of the 1916 Federal Employees' Compensation Act was afraid the government might be taken advantage of by shrewd claimants, and that's why he suggested a provision to circumvent excessive attorney fees negotiated by claimants; in third party lawsuits, that is—not necessarily in challenges to claim and benefit decisions, which were optimistically expected to be rare.[35] But the idea of interfering with a citizen's right to freely and independently contract for the services of a lawyer was controversial, so H.R. 15222's Section 29 provision did not carry over into H.R. 15316 and was not part of the law finally passed in 1916.[36]

In practice, OWCP automatically approves any attorney fee that isn't disputed by the claimant, as long as it isn't a contingency fee arrangement (one in which the attorney collects a percentage of the award rather than an hourly fee for rendered services). If a claimant disputes his or her attorney bill, OWCP evaluates those objections and either allows the charges to stand or revises them if they are deemed excessive.[37] The Employees' Compensation Appeals Board (ECAB) goes further, evaluating every non-trivial attorney fee application it receives, whether disputed or not.[38] On its website, the ECAB advises that "all fees for representative services performed in connection with an appeal before the Board require prior approval by the Board" and also that "an application for approval of a fee for services should not be submitted to the Board until after the appeal is closed."[39] Try telling an attorney you can't agree to pay his fee until you get a thumbs-up from the ECAB, and they won't look at it until all his work is done.

In Ohio, an attorney must disclose all fees received out of a BWC claimant's award, along with supporting evidence required to justify those fees, to the Industrial Commission for approval.[40] The good news for BWC claimants is that, if their appeals are elevated to a county court which then rules in their favor, they will be reimbursed reasonable attorney fees of up to $5,000 plus costs by either the employer or the Commission, whichever made the erroneous decision that was successfully contested.[41] This practice is only fair, since forcing employees to pay their own attorney fees even if their appeals are proven valid amounts to fining them for asserting their right to benefits and makes liberally denying claims a low-risk money-saving strategy for administrators.

As a matter of fact, it's a strategy that has been used before. By 1949, FECA benefits had fallen far behind increases in cost of living. The monthly wage replacement ceiling of $116.66 had represented two-thirds the salary of a letter carrier when last updated in 1927,[42] but by 1949 had slipped to less than one-half.[43] A package of amendments was produced which would raise that ceiling and improve benefits in various other ways as well. The proposed amendments, which contained no mention of attorney fees, were debated in the House of Representatives for four days in April and May of 1949, and then in the Senate for two days in June. The transcripts of those hearings[44] divulge only one brief conversation regarding attorney fees. Shortly into the April 11 session, the first day of hearings in the House, Congressman Thomas Werdel (R-CA) explained how the California workers' compensation system operated, with private insurance companies competing to provide coverage for businesses. He described a practice those insurers had of dragging out hearings on cases that appeared sure to be won by the claimant, with the intent of starving him out. Congressman Kenneth Keating (R-NY) chimed in, corroborating Mr. Werdel's observations as valid for his own state of New York as well.

> Mr. Werdel: ...the applicant, if there is no doubt at all in his claim, is given what is commonly known as the "rest cure." Then any attorney fees which he can receive in connection with the fight must come out of what he is to get. The result is that usually those people are very poorly represented.

Mr. Keating: That is right. The same is true in my State.

Mr. Werdel: I think it is generally true of all the States except one or two that allow an additional amount to be paid for attorney fees in connection with the same risk, and it is figured in. Now, when you get around to these items like subjective symptoms, of course, those things are always difficult to handle in any jurisdiction, and when you get to situations like amputations because of infection, you find the defense coming up with the fact that the person had eczema the year before, and that sort of thing.

Mr. Keating: That is right.

Mr. Werdel: And you have a long fight that the man cannot finance. I think that is one of the things that we ought to give thought to if we are going to amend the law. There is no point in having it appear that a man has provision made for representation and then not have it there, as a practical matter.

Mr. Keating: I agree that that is something that you ought to canvass if you are going into a complete revision of the workmen's compensation law.

The amendments as enacted on October 14, 1949 did not allow for additional award money to cover attorney fees, but the substance of Section 29 from the 1914 draft bill had reappeared, now in Section 23 of the FECA law: "No claim for legal services or for any other services rendered in respect of a case, claim, or award for compensation under this Act, to or on account of any person, shall be valid unless approved by the Administrator."[45] That change to Section 23 was slipped in by the House committee as a *technical*, rather than *substantive* amendment. Technical amendments normally consist of non-controversial edits such as corrections, clarifications, or supporting details used to perfect the wording of a law after all the substantive matters have been debated and formally decided. But in this case, the committee stretched the definition of "technical" open wide enough to insert two new prosecutable crimes. For one, new verbiage made it a misdemeanor punishable by up to $1,000, imprisonment up to one year, or both, for an attorney to solicit an injured worker's business with respect to a FECA claim or to collect a fee that hasn't been approved by the Administrator. The House wrote that "such a provision is necessary for the protection of claimants."[46]

Restricting the ability of attorneys to advertise their services to injured workers, or to profit significantly from their business, is bound to benefit workers in some scenarios but handicap them in others. The clear winner-every-time is the employer, who is sure to be spared some legal challenges thanks to suppressed advertising, and to face enervated challenges from underpaid attorneys. There is of course an inherent conflict of interests between legal representatives of injured workers and those of their employers, regardless of whether the parties are related as plaintiff vs. defendant under the old tort system, or beneficiary vs. benefit provider under a workers' compensation system. This rivalry was described colorfully by Minnesota Employees' Compensation Commissioner William McEwen in 1910:

> The Steel Corporation in our State has been so bothered with ambulance-chasing attorneys,—we have any number of them there, we know of over one hundred men in one county in Minnesota who make a living that way,—when an accident occurs in the mine, it is a question who will get there first, the claim agent of the company or the representative of the ambulance-chaser. The man who gets there first fixes up the evidence.[47]

The 1949 House committee made another "technical" amendment to Section 23 granting the FECA Administrator the right to prosecute any claimant who "disobeys or resists any lawful order or process, or misbehaves during a hearing or so near the place thereof as to obstruct the same," by taking the claimant to an actual court of law and charging him or her with contempt of court.[48] Unlike state workers' compensation claimants, FECA claimants have never been permitted to appeal claim-related decisions to any U.S. court. Prior to 1946, their only recourse was to request reconsideration by the same commissioners who had made the disputed ruling in the first place; since 1946, their appeals have been heard only by a panel of judges appointed by the same administrator who oversaw the original decision process. As of 1949, though still denied the benefit of a court hearing, FECA claimants can nonetheless be prosecuted for *contempt of court* in accordance with a criminal law that was enshrined by a technical amendment.

Ohio BWC fixes a claimant's attorney fee only in the event of controversy, so its approval process may generate a delay in payment but rarely a denial. Many states preemptively impose fee caps on lawyers representing workers' compensation claimants, expressed either as a maximum percentage of the claimant's award or dollar amount per hour of service. These limits have begun facing constitutional challenges in recent years. Restrictive attorney fee schedules were overturned in Florida and Utah in 2016, and Alabama in 2017. Proponents of the fee limits claim their intent is to prevent unsophisticated workers from paying too much for counsel, but in its written opinion, Utah's Supreme Court noted that the low fee limit in that state made many attorneys "economically unable or unwilling to take on injured workers' cases," a fact which reduced both the availability and quality of representation for workers.[49] Even good lawyers willing to represent them have an incentive to settle upon reaching the maximum fee allowed by law, putting workers at a disadvantage when arguing a case against lawyers representing administrators with no fee limitations.

As courts began calling foul on the paternalistic practice of limiting attorney fees payable by injured workers, the Department of Labor leapt into action. Perhaps in the spirit of "there's no defense like a good offense," it suddenly seemed very worried that it wasn't doing *enough* to protect injured civilians from predatory legal fees. The Labor Department's Office of Inspector General studied the matter and published its findings on March 31, 2016 in a report explicitly titled "OWCP and ECAB Did Not Monitor the Representatives' Fees Process to Protect FECA Claimants from Excessive Fees."[50] The report described an audit that had been conducted in response to "a Senate request that expressed concerns regarding the processes established to protect federal workers from paying excessive representation fees when they file workers' compensation claims."

No specifics were shared regarding who in the Senate was losing sleep over this situation, and what made him or her think claimants might be paying their lawyers too much, but the Inspector General's Office sallied forth in search of an answer and of course did not fail, pronouncing a verdict that "OWCP and ECAB did not ensure represented claimants and appellants were properly protected from paying excessive fees to their representatives." Findings from the audit were distilled into the following two statistics:

1. "OWCP did not obtain the required fee applications in 44 percent (12 of 27) of the OWCP claim files tested because OWCP did not notify claimants or their representatives of the requirement to file an application."

2. "ECAB notified appellants and their representatives of the requirement to file fee applications; however, less than two percent did so."

So, thanks to the Inspector General, we know that FECA claimants tend to ignore the attorney fee approval process, and it isn't enforced. The audit did not uncover a single instance of an exorbitant fee paid by a guileless claimant. It merely validated the universal truth that inefficient processes beg for circumvention. OWCP countered the Inspector General's critique with: "Given OWCP's lack of investigative resources and the long life cycle of many FECA claims, we are concerned that continuously monitoring fee approval compliance would require enormous resources that could adversely impact FECA benefit delivery to our injured workers."[51]

Shortly after publication of the Inspector General's report urging more consistent policing of attorney fees, OWCP received a call from an attorney who was owed $1,500 by one of his ex-clients, a correctional officer who had been injured in 2014. The attorney's fee application had languished in OWCP's queue for nearly a year, until he phoned in a reminder. OWCP approved it the next day. The claimant had since moved forward with a new attorney and was surprised to suddenly find himself on the hook for paying the old one. He filed an appeal. The ECAB heard his case and ruled that "as appellant agreed that the fees charged were fair and reasonable, OWCP did not abuse its discretion by approving the $1,500.00 fee for services rendered."[52] It almost makes you wonder what the point is of the approval process, doesn't it?

"So long as there is financial profit for any one in interpreting words for his own benefit, the proposed millennium in compensation acts—when both sides will be lawyerless, and written decisions will be unnecessary—will never be reached."[53]

-Samuel Horovitz, Attorney and worker advocate, 1944

CHAPTER 7

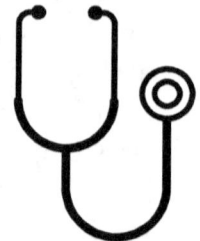

Is there a doctor in the house?

The employee is entitled under FECA to select the physician who is to provide treatment. The provider must meet the definition of "physician" under the FECA and must not have been excluded from payment under the program.

- Injury Compensation for Federal Employees, Publication CA-810

The morning of my injury, I was treated by my family doctor, who then referred me to a neurosurgeon. After undergoing back surgery and completing 12 sessions of physical therapy all before my workers' compensation case was approved, I assumed my family doctor would monitor my condition and manage any treatment I might need in the future. I was surprised to learn that she doesn't accept workers' compensation; she would go on treating me for anything else, but I was going to need a different doctor for my back. OWCP advertises that beneficiaries may choose any physician, and I had taken that assurance at face value, failing to consider that the choice is a two-way street; it doesn't do you much good to choose a physician who won't accept you as a patient.

I wasn't in dire need of further care at that point, but I hadn't made a full recovery, either; my back still ached most evenings, and I didn't know if that was something I just had to live with or a problem that could be solved. I decided to find a doctor who accepts federal workers' compensation; even if there was nothing any doctor could do for me right away, at least I'd have a ready provider in case my condition suddenly worsened, possibly sparing me a frantic search later. The welcome screen of OWCP's online provider search portal[54] warns that "the appearance of a specific medical provider's name in the listing does not require that provider to treat a particular claimant, even if OWCP has already advised the claimant in writing that medical treatment for a particular condition within the provider's listed specialty has been authorized." That turned out to be an understatement.

OWCP's provider portal interface is basic. Provider type and specialty are selectable from multiple choice menus cluttered with strange possibilities such as "rural hospital swing bed," "second opinion contractor," and "lien holder." A search can be delineated by city, state, or zip code, but there is no option to cover all areas within a given distance from a particular place such as home or work. A search for family physicians in my city yielded only seven practices. One treated only hospitalized patients, one was a facility that had closed the previous year, and two provided emergency care only. That left three possibilities. When I called them, two weren't accepting any new workers' compensation patients, and one of those didn't treat back injuries anyway. My last remaining option was Concentra, an occupational health care provider. I called and was relieved to hear that they were accepting new worker's comp patients. I tried to make an appointment, but the woman on the phone stopped me cold after hearing that my injury had occurred more than three months earlier. Concentra doesn't accept patients with injuries older than that because, as the woman cheerfully exclaimed to me over the phone, "We want to get you out!" That line certainly took me by surprise, and I didn't fully understand it until I learned that workers' compensation medical care providers are rated on measures that are single-mindedly focused on minimizing costs for employers and insurers (more about that in Chapter 12).

I repeated my search for a family practice physician in three nearby suburbs, reaping 11 hits total. One was a hospitalist group, three provided emergency care only, and two were urgent care centers.

That left five. I called them all. Four were not accepting any new workers' comp patients. The other one offered to treat me, but only if they could bill me or my private insurer and let us handle seeking reimbursement; they wouldn't deal directly with OWCP. By way of comparison, an online search for family doctors in my group health insurance network yielded 141 in my city proper, not counting any in outlying suburbs. Medicare's search engine offered up 131.

It is noteworthy that BWC, unlike OWCP, does not tell its beneficiaries they can initially choose any doctor they please. Instead, beneficiaries are restricted to BWC-certified providers.[55] On the surface, this might seem worse than OWCP's "choose any doctor" deal, but is it really? To find out, I searched BWC's provider look-up portal[56] for family practice physicians in my city. BWC offered 45 options, seemingly trouncing OWCP with its measly seven; however, that's largely because BWC lists each physician individually by name rather than lumping them together by practice as OWCP does. Among BWC's list of 45 possibilities were ten hospitalists, four emergency medicine providers, two urgent care providers, three who only offer outpatient services such as imaging and lab-work, four whose practices are permanently closed, two whose practices have moved, and four who specialize in areas unrelated to my injury. Still, that left 16 possibilities. I called them all. Ten were not currently accepting any new workers' comp patients. Two weren't accepting new patients at all. Three provided only short-term acute care (one of those was Concentra). I was down to one. I tried calling several times but waited on hold for ten minutes each time and never got through.

Although my simulated BWC search proved just as fruitless as my OWCP search had, BWC has a very significant point in its favor: It offers assistance to those who can't find a participating provider on their own. I can't say I tried that feature out—it might be just a mirage—but BWC does at least post this message on its search portal: "Note: While BWC has approved all providers listed within this look-up to do business with us, they may not be accepting new patients. If you need further assistance to find a provider, contact your managed care organization." In contrast, when I sent my OWCP case worker an email telling her I was having trouble finding a doctor, she didn't respond. In theory, OWCP's hands-off approach to doctor selection is a selling point over BWC; but in practice, OWCP beneficiaries have about the same (very limited) number of options and are at a serious disadvantage if they come up empty-handed. By technically not limiting your choice of providers, OWCP washes its hands of responsibility if you can't find one.

Two professors from the School of Medicine at UCLA studied the impact of medical fee schedules on willingness of providers to treat injured workers.[57] They found that in states where workers' compensation didn't pay much more than Medicare, doctors were far more willing to accept Medicare than workers' comp. The reasons most commonly given for shunning workers' comp patients were extreme paperwork demands along with a fee schedule that didn't adequately reimburse them for the extra work involved. Another driving factor was the frustration and uncertainty introduced by utilization review—the process whereby plan administrators evaluate and second-guess all requests for medical treatment on a case-by-case basis rather than publishing covered services and approval criteria as private insurers and Medicare do. Besides introducing a significant element of uncertainty, the utilization review process represents an extra step and delayed approval at best.

In an independent evaluation of Ohio BWC's medical care organizations, Deloitte Consulting LLC corroborated the findings of the UCLA study, attributing the stunted size of BWC's network to "provider resistance to participation due to fee schedules, [utilization review] constraints and administrative burdens."[58] Deloitte also reported significant bottlenecks in the process for medical treatment authorization, a reimbursement process that medical providers perceived as "burdensome," and fee schedules that hadn't been updated in five years. The great majority of physicians solve all those problems for themselves by simply refusing to accept workers' compensation patients.

An example of the extra paperwork demands levied upon doctors who treat workers' comp patients is Form CA-17, used by OWCP and federal employing agencies to obtain interim medical reports concerning a disabled employee's ability to return to light or full duty work. (BWC has a similar form, MEDCO-14.) The injured worker's supervisor fills out Part A of Form CA-17, describing the worker's physical job requirements in terms of how many continuous and intermittent hours per day involve lifting/carrying a specified weight, sitting, standing, walking, climbing, kneeling, bending, stooping, twisting, pulling, pushing, simple grasping, fine manipulation, reaching above the shoulder, driving a vehicle and operating machinery of specified types. The form also asks for environmental factors of the job such as continuous and intermittent exposure to temperature extremes, high humidity, chemicals and solvents of specified types, and noise level.

The employee next gives the form to the treating physician, who fills out Part B with medical findings, diagnosis, and an evaluation of the employee's ability to perform all the physical job activities defined in Part A on a full-time or part-time basis. The physician is also asked whether the patient's interpersonal relations are affected because of a neuropsychiatric condition. That's a lot to ask of a physician who may have only examined the patient once, in a non-work setting. While it's understandable that OWCP *wants* all that information, more often than not it's going to be impossible for the examining physician to provide it with any reasonable degree of certitude, forcing him or her to choose between playing a game of fill-in-the-blanks-with-baloney and refusing to treat workers' comp patients. Most choose the latter, and that doesn't seem to bother OWCP in the least.

The practice of requiring physicians to fill out a form on the federal claimants they treat dates back to 1918, when the U.S. Employees' Compensation Commission created a medical record card which contained a total of 14 questions and one line for remarks. Only two of the 14 questions required any familiarity with the claimant's occupation beyond basic facts such as place of employment, type of work, and name of supervisor. Question number 10 asked for "general medical or physical conditions bearing on case or prolonging disability," and yes-or-no question number 14 asked, "Is employee able to continue at his usual occupation without detriment?" In presenting their new card, the commissioners described it this way: "The card is 5 by 8 inches in size and has been made as simple as is compatible with the safe administration of the compensation act and the protection of the interest of both the employees and the commission."[59]

There ought to be a law that limits how much extra paperwork OWCP can dump on physicians who treat workers' compensation patients, and in fact there sort of is one. The Paperwork Reduction Act was passed in 1980 and revamped in 1995 to track and control the amount of paperwork imposed on the public by any federal agency, with the stated goal of ensuring "that Federal agencies balance their need to collect information with the paperwork burden imposed on the public in complying with the collection."[60] Every new or modified agency form or other information collection process must be reviewed by the Office of Management and Budget (OMB). An OMB control number is then assigned, which is required by law to be printed on the form, along with the form's purpose and estimated completion time, as part of a "public burden statement."

The public burden statement on Form CA-17 reads, "We estimate that it will take an average of 5 minutes to complete this collection of information, including time for reviewing instructions, searching existing data sources, gathering and maintaining the data needed, and completing and reviewing the collection of information." There's really no way an employer or physician could complete that form with meaningful responses in five minutes. It took me much longer than that to fill it out for myself, as I struggled to guess with any confidence how many continuous and intermittent hours a day I could sit, stand, walk, climb, kneel, bend, stoop, twist, etc.—especially considering that many of those activities might be sequential or combined, and "intermittent" could refer to moments or hours of rest in between. Why the OMB approved the flagrant underestimation of five minutes is anyone's guess, but it's of little practical importance since the Paperwork Reduction Act doesn't prohibit agencies from asking too much of anyone; it just requires them to obtain an OMB number first. Technically, the law also provides that no person may be penalized for refusing to fill out a federal form that doesn't have an OMB number printed on it, but if filling out the form is the only way to claim a benefit or allow employees or patients to claim a benefit, there's a built-in penalty for refusing to do so.

The UCLA study mentioned previously found that the hourly practice expense for physicians who accepted workers' compensation patients was 2.5 to 3 times the hourly Medicare practice expense.[61] Most workers' compensation systems pay providers more than Medicare does, but not 2.5 to 3 times more. Workers' compensation fee schedules generally allow payment of up to 1.5 times the Medicare limit for routine care; for instance, OWCP is currently willing to pay up to 1.34 times as much as Medicare, and BWC about 1.4 times as much, for office visits and physical therapy. For surgery, workers' compensation fee schedule limits are typically closer to twice the Medicare cap; for the back surgery my private insurer covered before my case was accepted, OWCP would have paid up to 1.6 times Medicare's going rate—assuming it would have authorized that surgery in the first place—and BWC pays up to 2.25 times the Medicare limit.[62]

In addition to having to process more paperwork and seek treatment approvals through a fickle utilization review process, workers' compensation doctors sometimes must coordinate with staff hired by the plan administrator to independently manage the patient's care. For instance, OWCP assigns field nurses to injured workers whose return to work appears uncertain—generally, these are claimants with disabilities lasting more than 45 days and subjective complaints of pain or limited motion. The field nurse attends key medical appointments with the injured worker, obtains relevant medical documentation and treatment notes for submission to OWCP, and facilitates meetings with the employing agency at the work site to discuss return-to-work opportunities. The nurse also provides the treating physician with a description of the physical requirements of the employee's job and presses for a work release returning the employee to full or light duty work.[63] Imagine how frustrating it would be for OWCP if it went to the trouble of twisting one doctor's arm only to have the worker switch to another. OWCP shrewdly avoids that predicament by requiring beneficiaries to obtain written approval first before changing physicians.

CHAPTER 8

'Til death do us part, Doc

Except for a referral made by the attending physician, any change in treat-
ing physician must be authorized by OWCP. Otherwise, OWCP will not
pay for the treatment. The employee should request any such change in
writing and explain the reasons for the request.

-Injury Compensation for Federal Employees, Publication CA-810

A FECA beneficiary can have only one physician of record at a time.
He or she may be referred by that physician to a specialist, but can't
change his or her primary physician of record without OWCP's
permission. According to 20 CFR 10.316, "OWCP will approve the
request if it determines that the reasons submitted are sufficient.
Requests that are often approved include those for transfer of care
from a general practitioner to a physician who specializes in treating conditions like the work-related one, or the need for a new physician when an employee has moved." I sought treatment on the
day of my injury from my family doctor, and I would have liked
for her to be my physician of record. Then workers' comp kicked in
and I discovered that she doesn't accept it. It wasn't clear to me
whether I needed permission to switch doctors anyway, and
whether I'd be committing myself indefinitely to a doctor I hadn't
met yet when I made the first appointment. I emailed those questions to my case worker, who chose not to reply. To its credit, Ohio
BWC has a policy of never denying a beneficiary's request to
change doctors.[64]

Having failed to find a family doctor to manage treatment of my back injury, I embarked on a new round of phone calls in search of an orthopedic specialist. The downside of choosing a specialist is that it locks me into one, whereas choosing a generalist would keep the door open for referrals to any number of specialists. Two of the OWCP-listed orthopedists I called didn't treat spinal injuries. One wasn't accepting new workers' compensation patients. Two were only accepting new workers' comp patients with injuries less than six months old. Two were accepting new workers' comp patients but asked me to bring a Form C-9 to my first visit. Form C-9 is used to request authorization for medical services from Ohio BWC. When I explained that I'm a federal employee and my benefits are provided through OWCP, which doesn't use Form C-9, I was instructed to bring them something similar, such as perhaps an "approval-to-treat" letter from OWCP. Knowing I had zero chance of conjuring such a thing, I moved on.

My next call felt like a miracle. Not only did the woman who answered the phone tell me her practice accepted workers' compensation patients without restrictions on time since injury, but she knew the difference between the federal and Ohio systems. She looked up my case number in some sort of database and instantly knew what type of injury I had sustained. Whatever slight discomfort I felt over the ease with which she found that information—and what else might be in the database and how many other people might have access to it—gave way to relief when she offered me an appointment. The doctor I saw ordered x-rays and an MRI to verify that my injury had healed properly (it had) and prescribed another round of physical therapy in a strongly worded way that won OWCP over. My therapy was approved, and I'm happy to say it helped a lot and I'm doing much better now. Not everyone is so lucky.

In 2014, a 28-year-old Navy materials engineer who is referred to as A.H. in a case summary published by the Employees' Compensation Appeals Board (ECAB) sustained multiple injuries when her vehicle was rear ended during work-related travel.[65] She sought medical treatment from her family physician, who diagnosed neck, lumbar, and left shoulder strain, as well as lumbar disc degeneration and upper back pain. A.H. was treated conservatively with chiropractic manipulations, physical therapy, muscle relaxants, and nonsteroidal anti-inflammatory drugs for over a year, during which time she experienced only mild improvement of her back pain and discomfort. She wanted more aggressive treatment in hopes of returning to her previous activity level, but her doctor continued to recommend pain management and activity restrictions instead of surgery. A.H. found this plan of action to be unacceptable. She wrote OWCP (twice) requesting permission to switch to a board-certified neurosurgeon she had found. OWCP denied the request, and she appealed. The ECAB heard her case and sided with OWCP in denying a change in treating physician, stating that "No transfer or termination of treatment should be made unless it is in the best interest of the claimant and the government."[66]

Declaring that employers owe their injured workers only medical care that has a direct payoff for the employer is a bold corruption of the Grand Bargain. It would be comforting to think the ECAB's ruling in A.H.'s case was an anomaly and not a reflection of its true philosophy; after all, conditioning a person's medical care on its value to her employer reduces her to the status of a farm animal. We treat our pets better than that, providing them with medical care for humane reasons and not because it's an investment we think we can recoup. But the same "best interest of the claimant *and the government*" rule appears in Chapter 3-0300 of the FECA Procedure Manual, which then goes on to suggest that transfer-of-care requests made by an injured worker's official superior will be considered.[67] Better start licking some boots at work if you don't like your doctor.

Here is how the ECAB justified telling A.H. that she was still a perfectly good engineer even with a bad back, and her employing agency didn't want to pay for surgery, so she had to either continue being seen by a doctor who wasn't helping much but at least wasn't costing much either, or switch to a doctor who might help more — and pay him herself:

> The Board has recognized that OWCP, acting as the delegated representative of the Secretary of Labor, has broad discretion in approving services provided under FECA. OWCP has the general objective of ensuring that an employee recovers from his or her injury to the fullest extent possible in the shortest amount of time. It, therefore, has broad administrative discretion in choosing means to achieve this goal. The only limitation on OWCP's authority is that of reasonableness. Abuse of discretion is generally shown through proof of manifest error, clearly unreasonable exercise of judgment, or actions taken which are contrary to both logic and probable deductions from established facts. It is not enough to show merely that the evidence could be construed to produce a contrary conclusion.[68]

A footnote was attached to the verbiage above, indicating that the ECAB was following precedent set in 1990 by Docket No. 90-1372.[69] That case involved letter carrier Daniel Perea, who was diagnosed in June 1987 by his family doctor with medial epicondylitis of the right elbow, a wear injury characterized by inflammation and pain due to overused tendons. His family doctor referred him to an orthopedic surgeon, who confirmed the diagnosis and also found evidence of nerve damage. Mr. Perea's condition worsened; by April 1988, his right arm was weakening, his left arm was becoming involved, and the pain had spread to his neck. His orthopedist referred him to a neurosurgeon who, based on symptoms and x-rays, suspected cervical stenosis (narrowing of the spaces between neck vertebrae) which could be pinching a nerve and radiating pain through Mr. Perea's neck and down his arms. An MRI performed in May 1988 revealed bulging and worn discs in Mr. Perea's cervical spine, for which the doctor recommended surgery.

OWCP sent Mr. Perea to another neurologist, Dr. Litvak, for a second opinion. Dr. Litvak noted damage to Mr. Perea's cervical spine but saw no "definite evidence of impingement upon the spinal cord" and attributed the pain in Mr. Perea's arms to carpal tunnel syndrome. He advised that more imaging studies were needed before he could support a decision to operate. To break the tie between Mr. Perea's doctor, who recommended surgery, and Dr. Litvak, who felt it wasn't warranted by the available evidence, OWCP brought in a third neurosurgeon, Dr. Friedman, who examined Mr. Perea and reported that "this patient clearly has evidence of cervical spondylosis which is probably in part symptomatic causing some radicular irritation in his right arm." Nevertheless, Dr. Friedman sided with Dr. Litvak, recommending that Mr. Perea be treated with more physical therapy, and if that didn't help, then more imaging studies should be done before surgery was undertaken. Consequently, OWCP denied Mr. Perea's request for surgery in November 1988, six months after it had been submitted.

Mr. Perea's neurosurgeon conducted the imaging studies recommended by Drs. Litvak and Friedman, which confirmed the presence of a herniated disc, so he again recommended surgery in February 1989, nine months after his initial request. OWCP again solicited the opinion of Dr. Friedman, who still argued against surgery after reviewing results of the imaging study, this time on the basis that the abnormalities in Mr. Perea's cervical spine didn't explain all of his symptoms. Mr. Perea's neurosurgeon and orthopedic surgeon both disagreed and resubmitted the authorization request for surgery. Mr. Perea consulted yet another neurologist, who also advised surgery. Those three medical opinions all fell on deaf ears; in April 1989, OWCP again denied authorization, "for the reason that the weight of the medical evidence, as represented by Dr. Friedman's reports, did not support a need for surgery."

Mr. Perea now had a lawyer, through whom he had requested an oral hearing with OWCP in December 1988 and again in January 1989, but his first request had been ignored and the second denied because "his case was not in posture for an oral hearing as the Office was in the process of reconsidering his request for surgery." With the surgery now officially shot down, Mr. Perea again requested a hearing. In the meantime, he consulted a physical medicine and rehabilitation specialist, who advised that he was not a candidate for pain rehabilitation because his right arm had atrophied, indicating a need for surgical intervention. Mr. Perea had an oral hearing with OWCP in August 1989. He testified with respect to his continuing symptoms and presented medical evidence of multilevel degenerative disc disease and a written statement from his neurosurgeon flatly refuting the statements of Dr. Friedman based on his own substantial experience treating patients with Mr. Perea's condition.

OWCP sent all the available evidence to Drs. Litvak and Friedman for review in September 1989, one year and four months after Mr. Perea's doctor had first recommended surgery. Dr. Litvak again diagnosed carpal tunnel syndrome to explain Mr. Perea's arm pain, dismissing the likelihood of any contribution from the multitude of undisputed defects in his cervical spine. Likewise, Dr. Friedman determined that there was "no evidence of any clearcut nerve root compression," though he admitted that Mr. Perea's "complaints at least in part do sound like they could be due to cervical nerve root irritation." Both second-opinion doctors still advised against surgery, but Dr. Friedman's stance had softened with time, and he wrote: "I would recommend that perhaps a third or fourth neurosurgical opinion be obtained because I feel that my opinion should not bar this patient from having surgery if he and his attending physician feel quite strongly about this."

But of course, Dr. Friedman's opinion *was* used by OWCP to bar Mr. Perea from having the surgery his treating physicians had all recommended—despite the fact that Dr. Friedman concluded his report with: "I am not holding myself forth as an absolute authority in this situation and am only giving him my opinion as to how I would personally approach his problem but that other opinions might well be equally valid." Mr. Perea appealed OWCP's refusal to authorize his surgery to the ECAB. In its written decision against him, the ECAB bowed to OWCP's "discretionary authority":

> The Office hearing representative found that the weight of the medical evidence regarding the likelihood of beneficial effects from the proposed surgery rested with the opinion of the impartial medical specialist, Dr. Friedman, who found surgery unnecessary. The Board finds that the Office did not abuse its discretionary authority in denying appellant's request for authorization of surgery.[70]

Much to his credit, ECAB Alternate Member Willie T.C. Thomas possessed enough character to dissent from that disgraceful majority rule and call OWCP out on its self-serving interference with medical care, writing: "Section 8103 of the Act does not give the Office authority to dictate to the treating physician the method or means of treating the employment injuries as long as the mean chosen by the treating physician comports with the accepted medical practices and meets the conditions specified under the Act."[71]

By the time Mr. Perea was granted his opportunity to appeal to the ECAB in November 1990, two years and six months had passed since his request for surgery had first been submitted to OWCP. He had endured the same sort of multi-year delay for which the old tort system was infamous; and like most injured workers under that archaic system, he had nothing to show for it in the end. On its website, the ECAB claims to conduct a *de novo* (i.e., new, unbiased) review of the cases it hears:

> The Board reviews all relevant questions of law and fact and questions involving the exercise of discretion. The decisions of the Board are based upon a full review of the case record upon which the Office rendered its decision to deny, award, or modify compensation benefits. In this regard, the Board conducts a de novo review of the case and is not limited to the terms of the

Office decision appealed from. The Board makes its own independent judgment of the relevant facts in an effort to reach a fair disposition of the issues supportable on the record.[72]

The ECAB may perhaps chart a de novo course when deciding eligibility for benefits, but it lowers the bar considerably when deciding matters over which it deems OWCP to have "broad discretion," such as provision of medical care. On that momentous topic, the ECAB openly admits to ruling by default in favor of OWCP and being swayed only if the appellant can prove "manifest error, clearly unreasonable exercise of judgment, or actions taken which are contrary to both logic and probable deductions from established facts." That is a far cry from "de novo." Not only can appellants not count on a timely or unbiased hearing, but according to the following words of warning on the ECAB website, they'd better come well-represented and prepared to wage exactly the kind of formal court battle the worker's compensation system was intended to spare them, with just as much as ever to lose but far less now to win:

It is generally recognized that benefits under the FECA in amount, duration and scope are among the highest under any workers' compensation statute. For this reason, appeals before the Board are often vigorously contested, extensively briefed, appellants represented by able private counsel or union representation, and oral arguments conducted in response to specific requests.[73]

"If, after making a claim, substantiated by a practicing physician in high standing, a claimant must abide by a decision founded upon the information of doctors and scientific men whom he does not know ... then the whole purpose of compensation laws as remedial legislation is defeated. The injured party had better far take his chances, as of old, either under liability or common-law procedure, where he would at least have the opportunity of meeting in open court those who would defeat his claim."[74]

-John Keegan, U.S. Employees' Compensation Commissioner, 1916

CHAPTER 9

Here's the deal

Unlike all other U.S. social insurance programs such as unemployment insurance, Social Security, and Medicare, no federal law sets minimum standards for workers' compensation benefits. OWCP has responsibility delegated to it by the Secretary of Labor for interpreting, enforcing, and administering the Federal Employees' Compensation Act. State workers' compensation programs have no federal funding or oversight and vary widely in terms of eligibility rules and benefits levels. States aren't required to even offer workers' compensation—though every state does, and every state besides Texas and Wyoming requires nearly universal coverage, exempting only small businesses, domestic or agricultural laborers, and independent contractors. Wyoming does not require coverage for approximately one-third of its employed citizens (those whose occupations are least hazardous). Texas has no coverage mandate at all. However, employers in both states who opt out of carrying workers' compensation insurance are subject to lawsuits by their employees and stripped of the original common law defenses, so most voluntarily purchase coverage.[75]

FECA and the state workers' compensation programs are all structured similarly but differ in specifics. A worker who is totally disabled, unable to work at all, receives wage replacement cash benefits equal to a certain percentage (typically 66 2/3%) of his or her pre-tax, pre-injury earnings, subject to minimum and maximum limits. Maximum weekly payments varied from $505 (in Mississippi) to $1,819 (in Iowa) in 2019. Most states impose waiting periods of three to seven days off work before wage replacement begins, but retroactively pay for that lost time if long-term disability ensues. Ohio has a seven-day wait, and its cash benefit limit of $980 per week was close to average among the states in 2019.[76] Federal employees have it better: FECA's 66 2/3% wage replacement rate is augmented to 75% for claimants who have dependents, and the upper limit is based on a high-end civilian salary—high enough so that it's rarely a true limiting factor. There is a three-day waiting period which applies to postal workers only.[77]

Most workers' compensation claims in the U.S. (62.5% in 2016) are for temporary total disability due to injuries or illnesses that require medical care only or limited time off work to recuperate but have no lasting effect. Though this type of claim is the most common, it garners a minor share of total benefits (33.7% in 2016). Conversely, only about 0.6% of claims typically involve death or permanent total disability, though together they commanded 9.6% of benefits in 2016.[78] Total disability is presumed permanent by both OWCP and BWC for workers who suffer the loss of (or lost use of) both hands or both arms, or both feet or both legs, or both eyes.[79] The FECA Manual cautions, "It does not mean, however, that a claimant in this medical condition should be automatically declared permanently and totally disabled. Some individuals may be able to work despite such severe medical conditions, and the possibility of rehabilitation and/or reemployment should be explored before any declaration is made."[80] FECA and most state programs continue to provide cash benefits to permanently, totally disabled beneficiaries either indefinitely or until they age into the Social Security system. However, some states cut payment off at a time limit (Mississippi is at the low end with a 450 week cap) or a monetary limit (Maryland is at the low end with a $45,000 cap).[81]

The most expensive category of claim is permanent partial disability; though only 36.9% of all 2016 claims fit this category, they accounted for 56.7% of total benefits paid.[82] An injured worker with a partial disability is able to work in some capacity but has an impairment that may reduce his wage-earning ability. OWCP and several states pay wage replacement benefits indefinitely to workers with permanent partial disabilities, but most states limit payment to a maximum number of weeks or dollar amount. There are a variety of methods used to determine compensation owed workers with lost wages due to a permanent partial disability. Some states replace a fixed percentage of the difference between actual wages before and after injury. Other states—and OWCP—estimate the claimant's earning *capacity* by medical exam or vocational assessment and substitute that value for actual post-injury earnings if it's higher. This practice reduces benefits for claimants who are not believed to be performing to their full potential. OWCP calls it "constructed employment" and has been making use of it with increasing regularity; the percentage of permanently, partially disabled federal civilians OWCP declared capable of earning more than they actually do rose from 35% in 2004 to 66% in 2012.[83]

Not all partial disabilities result in wage loss; for instance, an office worker who loses a leg might perform his or her job just as well as before. Some states calculate partial disability benefits based on overall impairment, without regard to either real or theoretical wage loss. Additionally, each state and OWCP has its own table of predetermined payments owed beneficiaries who lose specific body parts or use thereof. Such payments are commonly called "schedule awards." In general, OWCP's schedule awards compare favorably to BWC's. The highest award in either schedule is for loss of (or lost use of) an arm: OWCP deems it worth 312 extra weeks of pay, BWC only 225. Similarly, a federal employee's leg is worth 288 weeks of pay, while the going rate for a non-federal Ohio employee's leg is only 200 weeks. The only body parts OWCP and BWC value equally are the third, fourth, and fifth fingers—worth 30, 15, and 10 weeks of pay, respectively.[84]

In some respects, BWC is more generous than OWCP. If an injury causes serious disfigurement of the face, head, or neck, the BWC Administrator is authorized to make an additional benefit payment of up to $10,000. OWCP limits payment to only $3,500 under such circumstances, an amount which hasn't changed since it was added to the law in 1949, when $3,500 had the same spending power as more than $35,000 today.[85] If a worker dies of his or her injuries, OWCP pays up to $800 for funeral and burial expenses—a value that hasn't changed since 1966. Again, BWC does a better job of remaining current, paying up to $5,500 for funeral expenses.[86]

Both OWCP and BWC pay a percentage of a deceased employee's salary to a surviving spouse (at least until remarriage) and to children who are under the age of 18, full-time students, or incapable of self-support due to a disability. The percentage paid by OWCP depends on the mix of eligible dependents, ranging from 40% if there is no widow or widower and just one eligible child, to 75% if there is a surviving spouse and two or more eligible children. Spouses who remarry at age 55 or older continue receiving benefits.[87] Under BWC, all survivors share payments of 66 2/3% of the deceased employee's salary, subject to minimum and maximum limits.[88]

CHAPTER 10

The myth that workers' compensation is generous

In 1970, pervasive complaints about workplace safety inspired creation of the Occupational Safety and Health Act (OSHAct), which was signed into law by President Richard Nixon. The OSHAct created the Occupational Safety and Health Administration (OSHA) to serve as a regulatory authority for worksite safety, and the National Institute for Occupational Safety and Health (NIOSH) to research hazardous work conditions, provide education and training, and make recommendations for worker protections. The OSHAct also created the National Commission on State Workmen's Compensation Laws to investigate concerns about the fairness and effectiveness of those laws. The National Commission had 18 members: three from Nixon's Cabinet and the rest appointed by him from among representatives of state workers' compensation boards, insurance carriers, business, organized labor, the medical profession, educators, and the general public.

The National Commission was directed to "undertake a comprehensive study and evaluation of state workmen's compensation laws to determine if such laws provide an adequate, prompt, and equitable system of compensation."[89] It began this task by identifying five objectives for workers' compensation:

1. broad coverage of employees and of work-related injuries and diseases;

2. substantial protection against interruption of income;

3. provision of sufficient medical care and rehabilitation services;

4. encouragement of safety; and

5. an effective system for delivery of the benefits and services.

After two years spent evaluating state laws against those five major objectives, the National Commission presented its findings and recommendations to the President and Congress in 1972, reporting: "Our intensive evaluation of the evidence compels us to conclude that State workmen's compensation laws are in general neither adequate nor equitable."[90] That outcome was all but inevitable. From the very start, there has been tremendous variability in benefit levels and administrative rules among the state (and federal) programs; and as Dr. I.M. Rubinow pointed out in 1917, "absence of uniformity necessarily presupposes absence of adequacy in some acts, since it may be safely assumed that definitely excessive standards, as compared with the economic loss sustained, can hardly be expected."[91]

The Commission made 84 specific recommendations in total, 19 of which it deemed "essential." The essential recommendations sought compulsory rather than elective coverage, fewer exempted categories of employees, inclusion of diseases as well as injuries, adequate wage replacement and death benefits, and no arbitrary time or spending limits on medical and rehabilitation benefits, or on wage replacement for total disability cases. The mostly Republican commission rejected federalization of state workers' compensation programs, but unanimously supported the enactment of federal standards as needed to achieve compliance with the 19 essential recommendations. National Commission Chairman John F. Burton, Jr. later wrote:

> How could a National Commission dominated by Republicans unanimously conclude that state laws were "in general neither adequate not equitable" and that Congress should enact Federal standards for state workers' compensation programs if states did not significantly improve their laws?

First, most members were experts in workers' compensation and cared about the future of the program. The hearings and evidence presented to the National Commission revealed a system in much worse shape than these experts had expected, and they were willing to open their minds to fundamental changes in order to preserve the state-run system.[92]

The Commission proposed giving states three years to improve, then conducting a 1975 review of compliance, after which federal mandates should be imposed to close any remaining gaps. Immediately following publication of the National Commission's report, a combination of increased awareness, public pressure, and threat of regulation prompted most states to revise their laws in favor of better benefits. The recommended follow-up review lost its sense of urgency; it didn't happen in 1975 as planned, and by the mid-1980s, when it became clear that it wasn't likely to ever happen, progress faltered. By the early 1990s, public attention had moved along to new topics, and it became safe once again for workers' compensation benefit providers to shift their own focus away from quality and fairness, back to controlling costs. Weakening labor unions and other employee advocates were unable to hold back the tide as legislation was introduced in most states that chipped away at benefits and created new hurdles to claiming them.[93] As described in a report by the Department of Labor:

> Various new legislative changes were championed as "reforms." It was a race to the bottom: as each state compared its statute with those of neighboring states, found areas of greater generosity, and moved to change those provisions of its law.[94]

Workers' compensation doesn't replace all of an injured worker's financial losses, nor was it meant to. Workers are squeezed by waiting periods, benefit caps, lost opportunities for advancement, lost income from second jobs, overtime and shift differentials, loss of home production, and lawyer fees for disputed claims. This is all in addition to pain and suffering and loss of ability to participate in hobbies and other non-work activities. A study of ten-year outcomes for beneficiaries whose injuries resulted in permanent partial disability found that the percentage of pre-tax income replaced by workers' comp fell far short of the targeted 66 2/3%, ranging from a high of 46% in New Mexico to a low of 29% in Wisconsin.[95] A formal analysis taking into account all the direct and indirect costs of workplace injuries concluded that employers foot, on average, only about 21% of the total bill. Workers and their private health insurers pay 63%, and the other 16% is shifted to taxpayer-funded programs such as Medicare and Medicaid.[96]

As for medical benefits, lack of consistency and transparency makes it difficult to compare the standards of care delivered by workers' compensation programs either to those of other such programs or to the defined standards guaranteed by private insurance plans and Medicare. For that matter, there is no assurance that two beneficiaries under the same workers' comp system will receive the same standard of care. One of the conclusions published in the Deloitte assessment of Ohio BWC was that "lack of standardization had the potential to result in inconsistent [Utilization Review] decisions regarding accepted or denied care with all other claim and claimant characteristics being equal. This is a common scenario among state systems."[97] The same concern applies to federal systems managed by OWCP: Are some claims examiners more generous than others? Do physical laborers get more extensive rehabilitation services than office workers? Is it easier to get treatments approved at the beginning of a fiscal year when budgets have been topped off? We shouldn't have to wonder.

OWCP has an online Medical Bill Processing Portal[98] for medical authorization requests, bill submission, and provider payment status. Curious to see if treating my injury had cost my employer any more than it had likely saved by not clearing ice from the parking lot, I logged into the system and reviewed the status of my medical bills. OWCP had reimbursed my group health insurer for all my physical therapy sessions, a visit to my primary care physician on the day of my injury, x-rays, an MRI, and surgical consultations and follow-up visits. However, it had reimbursed only $9.58 of my $7,083.71 surgical bill. That surgery made a world of difference, relieving most of my pain and enabling me to stand up straight again; I hate to think what my life would be like today if my insurer had denied it.

I was surprised to realize that OWCP may deny any medical procedure to any beneficiary just by disagreeing that it's needed. A denial can be appealed, but that takes time – and money, too, if a lawyer's help is needed. A casual look at FECA law regarding provision of medical care might make a lawyer cringe but wouldn't raise more than a few hairs on the back of the average person's neck. In fact, the open-ended wording used can create the impression that FECA is *more* generous than private insurance plans or Medicare, which publish finite lists of covered services. Below are excerpts from FECA law regarding provision of medical care, with the giant loophole language underlined.

Federal statutory law in Title 5, Section 8103 of the U.S. Code states:

> **5 U.S.C. 8103. Medical services and initial medical and other benefits**
>
> (a) The United States shall furnish to an employee who is injured while in the performance of duty, the services, appliances, and supplies prescribed or recommended by a qualified physician, which the Secretary of Labor considers likely to cure, give relief, reduce the degree or the period of disability, or aid in lessening the amount of the monthly compensation.

Federal administrative law in Title 20, Section 10.310 of the Code of Federal Regulations states:

> **20 CFR 10.310. What are the basic rules for obtaining medical care?**

(a) The employee is entitled to receive all medical services, appliances or supplies which a qualified physician prescribes or recommends and <u>which OWCP considers necessary</u> to treat the work-related injury.

Ohio Revised Code (ORC) Section 4123.66 contains similar wording which applies to BWC:

ORC 4123.66. Making additional payments for medical or funeral expenses.

(A) In addition to the compensation provided for in this chapter, the administrator of workers' compensation shall disburse and pay from the state insurance fund the amounts for medical, nurse, and hospital services and medicine <u>as the administrator deems proper</u> and, in case death ensues from the injury or occupational disease, the administrator shall disburse and pay from the fund reasonable funeral expenses in an amount not to exceed fifty-five hundred dollars.

Explicitly allowing workers' compensation administrators carte blanche to decide how much medical care they owe injured workers is a breathtakingly naive concession. It's a power that was first spelled out in FECA law nearly a century ago, before the advent of managed care, back when doctors routinely did all they could for their patients; and its original intent was benevolent – to ensure no one could interfere with the administrator's decision to authorize medical care of any kind (see Chapter 20). Today it serves the opposite purpose, empowering the administrator to veto doctor recommendations and deny medical treatment with impunity.

Patrice Woeppel, Ed.D., describes the aftermath of her own workplace injury in her book *Depraved Indifference*. Patrice sustained a neck injury from slipping on a dirty floor in the hospital where she worked as a director, then encountered a relentless series of obstacles in her quest to obtain medical care through her employer's workers' compensation program. She was initially denied an x-ray or MRI or any other type of diagnostic evaluation. When her primary care physician referred her to a neurologist who accepted workers' comp and who offered her an appointment, coverage for the visit was denied on no other grounds than that it would be "too costly."[99] She found herself in an agonizing limbo between workers' compensation, which continually denied medical treatment, and her private health insurer, which wouldn't cover treatment because the injury had happened at work. She writes: "For two years all treatment, all therapy, all prescriptions, were denied by the insurer. My life became centered on how to get comfortable — a snatched few moments lying very still."[100]

The Ohio BWC Ombuds Office 2015 Annual Report divulged a particularly harrowing account of a worker who had sustained a spinal cord injury that left him with no use of his arms and legs. BWC declared him permanently and totally disabled and then proceeded to fight having to pay for modifications to make his home handicapped accessible, and to deny several of his prescribed medications, delay provision of necessary and time sensitive medical supplies, and resist paying his medical bills. Ombudsmen intervened numerous times to help him fight these battles, but still his situation went from bad to worse. He made a frantic call to the Ombuds Office because he had been abandoned home alone by his home health care service; no one was there to change his catheter or reposition him to prevent bedsores. An investigation traced the problem to BWC's policy of covering home health services for at most eight hours per day. A temporary exception had been made for this quadriplegic man, but BWC's gesture of goodwill had expired and the form to renew it was pending. The Ombuds Office intervened yet again to get his home health care services restored.[101]

CHAPTER 11

Continuous improvement

If you've never heard the phrase "continuous improvement," chances are you've been out of the workforce for a while. No matter what you do for a living, your employer most likely measures your performance in some way and urges you to do "better" this year than last.

In its Fiscal Year 2018 (FY18) report, BWC proudly shared this announcement:

> BWC paid providers nearly $531 million for medical and vocational services during FY18, which is $18.3 million less than payments made in FY17. For FY17 BWC paid $549.3 million, which is $29.5 million less than payments made in FY16.[102]

Its Fiscal Year 2016 report contained a similar boast:

> For medical and vocational services rendered during Fiscal Year 2015 (FY15), as of early November 2015, BWC paid providers nearly $612.5 million, which is $45.1 million less than the payments made in FY14. For FY16, as of early November 2015, BWC paid $582.5 million, which is $30 million less than payments made in FY15.[103]

Of course, what BWC paid is more-or-less what injured workers received, so those trends are either impressive or ominous, depending on your perspective. Either way, it's clear that the BWC

Administrator, like most of us, is under pressure to show continuous improvement.

In Fiscal Year 2011, BWC established a formulary, or list of approved medications, to "improve the efficiency and effectiveness of treatment, limit the inappropriate use of medications and lower BWC's prescription costs."[104] In Fiscal Year 2016, BWC reported spending $46 million less on prescription drugs than it had in Fiscal Year 2011—a dazzling 34% reduction.[105] It's not uncommon for workers' compensation administrators to achieve prescription drug savings any private health insurer would envy. The National Council on Compensation Insurance (NCCI), an advisory service for workers' comp insurers, reports that nationwide in 2011, an average of 67.6% as much money was spent on medications for injured workers whose treatment was managed and paid for within a workers' comp network as compared to those who received care out-of-network. By 2016, that ratio had crept down to 54.4%. The NCCI tactfully spins this difference in favor of workers' comp by reckoning that maybe it means in-network doctors exercise greater caution in prescribing opioids, which are a major cost driver, or have better access to non-opioid treatment options.[106] Of course, there's also the more obvious explanation that freedom from the damping forces of market pressures and government regulation makes showing "continuous improvement" in workers' compensation expenditures as easy as taking candy from a baby.

The NCCI reports that prescription drug prices, on the whole, increased over the span from 2011 through 2016. Savings, where they occurred, were due entirely to reduced utilization.[107] What we don't know is how much of that reduced utilization was due to there being fewer severe injuries, how much was due to doctors prescribing fewer or less expensive medications based on their own best judgment, and how much was due to prohibitions and paperwork hurdles imposed by BWC. BWC explains in its Fiscal Year 2019 report what it demands of doctors who prescribe opioids, and why: "If prescribers are not compliant with the documentation requirements, they are sent a series of letters requesting the missing documentation. After multiple requests, if BWC does not receive the documentation, payment for opioids prescribed by that provider will no longer be reimbursed. The purpose of this rule is to ensure BWC only reimburses for opioid medication when best practices are followed by the prescriber. This keeps the safety and health of our injured workers a top priority."[108]

In Fiscal Year 2019 relative to Fiscal Year 2018, Ohio BWC saved a disproportionate 20.2% in pharmacy costs by allowing 8.9% fewer prescriptions, suggesting that the medications targeted for reduced prescribing were the more expensive ones.[109] Of course, it's possible those just happen to be the same ones BWC sincerely believes pose a threat to their "top priority"—the safety and health of Ohio's injured workers—but BWC reports nothing about outcomes for those workers beyond how much less medicine they're getting and how much money it's saving BWC. There's an implied supposition that all the medication being denied to them isn't really needed and therefore they're better off without it; but we don't know how many thrive under BWC's increasingly austere prescribing regimen and how many suffer needlessly.

The 2015 BWC Ombuds report tells of an injured worker whose prescription was denied by his pharmacy. The man had appealed BWC's original denial of his medication to the Industrial Commission, which ruled in his favor. Yet his medication was still being denied. The Ombuds Office traced the problem to an incorrect interpretation by a BWC nurse and requested that it be reviewed by a supervisor. By this time, the injured worker was reporting suicidal thoughts. The ombudsperson helpfully suggested he contact a medical health professional about that and went back to untangling the medication approval thread. Ultimately, BWC acknowledged that the man's medication should have been approved and corrected the status so his pharmacist was able to fill it.[110] In a similar incident reported in 2014, the owner of an Ohio company called the Ombuds Office to complain that he was "extremely frustrated that his employee was not getting what he needed in order to heal and work without restrictions." Then he handed the phone over to the employee, who told the ombudsperson "he was at a breaking point because he was in so much pain but did not want to be off work." Again, the Ombuds Office traced the problem to confusion within BWC and was able to get the man's medication approved.[111]

Just as states compare their benefits favorably to those of other states to help justify cuts, proponents of FECA benefit cuts point out areas in which FECA is more generous than the states. When cuts are made, they are euphemized as "improvements," "enhancements," or "reforms." During a 2013 hearing before Congress on Bill H.R. 2465, a proposed "Federal Workers' Compensation Modernization and Improvement Act," comparisons to less generous state benefits were offered repeatedly as justification for reducing FECA benefit levels.[112] Gary Steinberg, OWCP's Acting Director at the time, asserted without evidence that FECA's superior benefit levels "create direct disincentives to return to work." He boasted of $53 million saved over the previous ten years as a result of "significant strides in disability management" that had translated into 20% fewer workdays lost due to serious injuries. He hoped to build on that success with this new package of FECA amendments that would save the government a projected $500 million over the next ten years. Sadly for Mr. Steinburg, H.R. 2465 was torpedoed by an analysis the Government Accounting Office presented which exposed the extent of the harm it would have done: OWCP's bid to join the states in their race to the bottom via H.R. 2465 would have left the median totally disabled federal employee with a third less retirement income than if he or she hadn't been catastrophically injured at work.[113]

Because of how nebulous the medical care aspect of FECA law is, OWCP has quite a bit of administrative latitude to adjust benefit levels downward without going through Congress. On its website, OWCP published news about recent "enhancements" to its medical authorization and billing system. Skip to the last sentence to see what it means to injured civilians.

Enhancements to OWCP's Medical Authorization and Billing System

We have recently enhanced our computer system to ensure that the care the injured worker is receiving is relevant to the condition(s) for which the case was accepted. These enhancements were made in accordance with the Federal Employees' Compensation Act which mandates OWCP to furnish an injured worker with services, appliances, and supplies prescribed by a qualified physician which OWCP deems likely "to cure, give relief, reduce the degree or the period of disability, or aid in lessening the amount of monthly compensation." While we have always had processes in place to help assure that OWCP authorizes and pays only for services, treatments, medications, and durable medical equipment related to the accepted conditions on a claim, our recent computer enhancements provide more rigor to these processes.

As a result of this, some injured workers may find that treatment or medications previously allowed are no longer available to them.[114]

Workers' compensation insurers and private health insurers alike are motivated to minimize expenditures, but there is this vital difference: If a private health insurer cuts benefits by too much, it will lose customers, and if it loses too many customers, it will go out of business. Workers' compensation insurers have no such worries — beneficiaries do not have the luxury of switching to another; they await the edict of their preordained benefit administrator like insects pinned to a board. Meanwhile, an employer's immunity from lawsuits is absolute, not lost or gained by degree in accordance with how much he or she pays into the system; employers with low premiums are just as impervious as those with high premiums. Thus, the insatiable appetite of employers and administrators for cost reduction is not tempered by any potential loss as it would be if free market rules applied.

If injured workers can't count on government regulation or market pressures to guard their interests, they must depend on the kindness and good character of complete strangers. That hasn't always been such an unrealistic bet. On April 21, 1926, Bessie Brueggeman and Charles Verrill appeared before Congress.[115] Mrs. Brueggeman was chairperson of the three-person commission that administered FECA back then, and Mr. Verrill was a member. They had brought along their disbursing officer, E.V. Parker, because they were there to ask for more money. The appropriations hearing was chaired by Martin Madden, and to say the least he wasn't pleased when Mr. Parker presented him with an itemized statement demonstrating a budget deficit of $226,900. Naturally, Chairman Madden was interested in knowing how that had happened.

> The Chairman: Have you any control over these expenditures?
>
> Mr. Parker: No, sir.
>
> The Chairman: Or are they made in accordance —
>
> Mr. Parker (interposing): With the number of cases that come before us and are passed upon by the commission.

Mr. Madden proceeded to grill the commissioners on how they decided whether to accept any given claim and how they determined the amount of compensation due. The court recorder produced a transcript of the inquiry spanning fifteen pages before Mr. Madden reluctantly acquiesced. Near the end of her testimony, Mrs. Brueggeman assured him, "We do not like to come down and ask for a deficiency." He retorted, "We would rather you would not."

"And we would rather not do it," Mrs. Brueggeman reiterated.

And yet they did it. The committee had broad discretion and could easily have stayed within budget or even shown "continuous improvement" simply by denying more and more claims. They could have avoided all the unpleasantness of that day and instead held themselves up as shining examples of budgetary restraint. Yet they set aside their self-interests and acted with integrity and un-compromising fairness. Imagine that, can you?

CHAPTER 12

Trickle-down medical care

In September 2017, Florida resident Neil Eckelberger suffered severe injuries and burns in an explosion at his workplace. He was well-cared-for in the hospital for ten days, then returned home to a rude awakening. With the emergency phase of treatment behind him, Travelers, his employer's workers' compensation insurance carrier, would not approve follow-up visits to any of the doctors recommended by hospital staff. During the ten weeks it took them to identify a doctor he *could* see, he had to use a walk-in clinic. Travelers later denied treatment for his back injury and testing for the traumatic brain injury suspected by the very doctors it had approved him to see. When questioned by a reporter about the quality of care provided to Mr. Eckelberg, a Travelers spokesperson responded: "Our goal is to ensure that each injured employee receives the best care available...so they can recover as quickly as medically appropriate and return to work."[116]

Pam Ferrandino, representing workers' comp insurer Willis North America, sang a similar tune in a *Leader's Edge* article published the previous year: "I think most employers are focused on preventing injuries, but when events do happen, it is getting the employee treated with the best level of care so that they can return to work quickly."[117] A well-loved and well-worn narrative among workers' compensation benefit providers is a sort of medical care version of trickle-down economics—the notion that doing what's best for employers automatically serves the best interests of injured workers as well. After all, employers want their injured employees back at work as soon as possible, right? And the sooner those employees recover, the sooner that can happen, right? And better medical care should correlate to a faster recovery, right? Ergo, employers are intrinsically motivated to provide their injured employees with top-notch medical care…

…except maybe the ones with desk jobs, who can be just as productive with a physical disability…and the ones with minor injuries, who will heal just fine even with very basic or delayed care……and the ones who are so badly hurt it would be cheaper to reassign them to sedentary jobs or write them off altogether than to heal them……and the ones who are close to retirement……and the ones with subjective complaints who can't prove they're unable to do their jobs, so there's a legal basis for telling them they either return to work immediately or they're fired……and the ones with private insurance who will be more likely to use it even for work-related injuries and diseases if that's easier and less stressful than going through workers' compensation.

In general, the easier and more worthwhile it is for injured workers to recover lost wages and obtain medical care through workers' compensation, the more likely they are to do so rather than take sick leave and either forgo medical care, pay for it out of pocket, or use private health insurance. This is not mere speculation—a number of studies showed that when state and federal workers' comp benefits became more generous in the 1970s and early 1980s, the dollar amount of benefits paid out surged beyond expected levels because more claims were filed and the average duration of claims increased.[118] It is decidedly *not* in the best interests of employers and insurers to provide a generous level of workers' compensation benefits, and they certainly know it. The aggressively promoted falsehood that it's what they *want* to do diverts attention from the disconcerting fact that they don't *have* to do it; the only true limiting factor in their game of "how low can you go" is an ability to put a good enough spin on what they do or don't do to keep the public from recognizing the need for intervention.

Provision of medical care to injured workers has long been posed as a self-serving practice for employers. Inclusion of medical aid as a workers' compensation benefit in addition to wage replacement was brought up for consideration by George M. Gillette, a member of the Minnesota Employees' Compensation Commission, at a Conference of Commissions held in Chicago in November 1910. Mr. Gillette pointed out to his colleagues that it "is for the interest of the employer to see that that man from the very start of his injury has the very best sort of hospital care and surgical attendance. Otherwise, very serious consequences might flow from the ill care of injury." Conference Chairman H.V. Mercer concurred: "It would seem to me, after my experience in Europe, that it might be a business proposition from the employer's standpoint, to take care of the hospital bills and the doctor's bills during the first two weeks free of charge. I think he would make money out of it in the end."[119]

Wisconsin distinguished itself early on by stipulating in its 1911 act that medical care must be provided not only to *cure*, but also to *relieve* the injured worker. In the text of its 1913 revised act, the Wisconsin Industrial Commission justified expanding medical coverage to include hospital stays by starting down the cynical, well-trodden path of enlightened self-interest, then veering onto higher ground at the last moment:

> Where the injured workman receives full and competent medical attendance he is able to return to work sooner, and many injuries which might otherwise result very seriously are quickly cured and compensation ceases. Under our act the cost of medical attendance is high, but there should be, and we think there is, a corresponding saving in compensation. At any rate the provision is humane and just.[120]

Similarly, U.S. Employees' Compensation Commissioner Charles Verrill tried the business ledger line of reasoning out on Congress in 1926, but didn't get far with it before being pulled up short by New York Representative Nathan Perlman:

> Mr. Verrill: ...It is a business proposition. A man is disabled, and you pay him as long as he is disabled, according to his disability. If you do not take steps to cure him, you add to the amount of compensation that you pay. If you do not give him all the treatment and care and appliances that are needed to get him back to work, you pay for it in compensation, at the compensation rate. It is a good deal cheaper to cure, if you can, than it is to pay compensation.
>
> Mr. Perlman: It is much more humane to cure him, of course.[121]

It may seem harmless enough to sell employers on the idea of providing a decent standard of medical care to their injured employees by suggesting it will ultimately help their bottom line, but as Dr. Rubinow cautioned in 1917, "It is one thing to shape legislation so as to make use of this economic motive to obtain socially desirable results, and quite another to depend upon it exclusively to accomplish what is desirable. The average adjuster of claims may not be enlightened enough to see the far-reaching results of such liberal medical treatment, and the stimulus to keep the medical cost down to the lowest legal limit must in most cases be overwhelming. Moreover, one would scarcely want to depend entirely upon someone else's economic motive for the preservation of health and limb, nay, even life."[122]

Dr. Rubinow's early distaste for the enlightened self-interest lure was shared by John B. Andrews, Secretary of the American Association for Labor Legislation in 1912, who wrote: "Recently a few of the less thoughtful enthusiasts in the popular agitation for efficiency have failed to get the true perspective and have clamored for protection for the workers solely upon the ground that 'it pays' the employer. Let us congratulate ourselves that those who are in danger of losing their health and their lives in their daily toil have in some instances at least that incidental advantage. But let us have less of this everlasting dinning in our ears that, before we ask for decent protection for the workers, we must first demonstrate that each advance toward health and safety will actually put additional dollars in the pockets of employers."[123]

When an injured employee needs medical care, the best possible outcome for his employer and workers' comp insurer is if someone else (such as the employee or his private insurer) pays for it. This is obviously and objectively true and no reflection on anyone's ethics. Workers' comp administrators are rewarded for repelling and losing as much "business" as possible. The more difficult they make the process for injured workers to obtain approval of claims for wage replacement and medical treatment, the better their metrics of "success" become. Attorney James Linehan, OWCP hearings officer-turned-whistleblower, testified in 2000 to the House Committee on Government Reform. The excerpt below is from the published report on those proceedings[124]:

> According to Mr. Linehan, there is no incentive, legally or economically, for the OWCP to act in the "best interest" of the Federal employee. In reality, quite the opposite occurs. It is in the "best interest" of the OWCP and the employing Federal agency to delay, stall or deny claims because such non-action saves the OWCP from claims payments. In effect, Mr. Linehan stated, this lack of accountability by the OWCP has directly led to the rapidly growing refusal of qualified medical practitioners across the United States to medically treat injured or diseased Federal civilian employees. The OWCP mandates that it must pre-approve and authorize medical treatment, however, the OWCP is under no timeline requiring it to issue such approval and authorization for medical treatment. The injured Federal worker who needs immediate medical treatment must first find a physician who will treat him or her. But physicians are highly reluctant to accept the cases because

they are aware that they may not be paid for months, years, or at all by the OWCP. In addition, Mr. Linehan stated that there are less than a handful of practicing attorneys across the United States who will represent Federal civilian employees in their workers' compensation claims because there is no court review. "No review means no payment," he said.

Without accountability, Mr. Linehan stated, the OWCP is free to act in any manner it desires toward an injured Federal civilian employee. The OWCP is free to refuse to respond to claimants' telephone calls; free to refuse to acknowledge receipt of correspondence or medical records from claimants or their physicians; and is free to delay or wrongfully deny due compensation benefits to the claimant.

In 1984, Eliyahu M. Goldratt and Jeff Cox published a book titled "The Goal," which has since been revised and republished several times.[125] A central message of the book is that rarely is an organization's true goal accurately expressed by its mission/vision statement. Some examples of raison d'êtres professed by major companies include:

Amazon: "Serve consumers through online and physical stores and focus on selection, price, and convenience"

Google: "Organize the world's information and make it universally accessible and useful"

Walmart: "Save people money so they can live better"

All for-profit companies actually have the same goal: to make money. There's nothing wrong with that, but it needs to be acknowledged in order to make sense of corporate behavior.

Government agencies all have a variation on that goal: to execute their assigned duties with optimal efficiency; that is, with as little expenditure as possible of time and money. Again, this just needs to be acknowledged in order to make sense of an agency's behavior.

OWCP claims its mission is "to protect the interests of workers who are injured or become ill on the job, their families and their employers by making timely, appropriate, and accurate decisions on claims, providing prompt payment of benefits and helping injured workers return to gainful work as early as is feasible."[126] Similarly, Ohio BWC proclaims: "Our vision, to transform BWC into an agile organization driven by customer success. Our mission, to deliver consistently excellent experiences for each BWC customer every day."[127] Those are nice words and perhaps heartfelt, but the truth is, OWCP and BWC weren't borne out of someone's burning desire to help injured workers. They were created because federal and state laws were passed *requiring* that benefits be paid to injured workers; OWCP and BWC are tasked with satisfying those legal requirements, and they're expected to do so as inexpensively as they can.

For a clear view of an organization's goals, there is no more transparent lens than their metrics. It takes time and costs money to collect data. People generally measure what they care about and only what they care about. Ohio BWC grades each of its Managed Care Organizations annually and publishes an "MCO Report Card."[128] Here are the criteria against which MCOs are judged:

* Total days of work missed by injured employees
* Recent medical costs
* Timeliness in submitting claims to BWC
* Promptness and accuracy in payment of provider bills
* Employer satisfaction

The employer satisfaction survey was introduced in 2018. You'll notice there is no claimant satisfaction survey. One of the recommendations that came out of the 2009 Deloitte study funded by BWC was to survey injured workers about their medical care outcomes. Deloitte described such surveys as a key measure of utilization review performance and noted that "constituent surveys also promote a high level of transparency that is important in publicly administered programs."[129] Unfortunately, collecting and reporting claimant survey data would be problematic for BWC because a claimant's goals are fundamentally at odds with the behaviors for which MCOs are rewarded: providing cheap medical care and rushing him back to work.

MCOs post slogans on their websites that are geared toward employers, not employees:

1-888OhioComp: "Premium reduction is not by accident"[130]

3-hab: "One of our larger clients saved $309,725.48 in medical costs and 3,479 in lost days over one year!"[131]

Occupational Health Link: "Our focus is on providing quality care that is affordable and returning your workers to work as swiftly as possible."[132]

Just as an employer's priorities are implicitly attached to the money it pays workers' comp administrators, so do administrators pass those priorities on to their provider network. Recall from Chapter 7 that I was able to find only *one* primary care provider in my city or surrounding suburbs willing to accept new workers' compensation patients, and that was Concentra. But Concentra wouldn't give me an appointment because my injury had occurred more than three months prior to my call. The reason that mattered to them is plain to see from this boast on their website: "Only 7% of Concentra injury cases are recommended to be off-duty, compared to a 30% national average. We treat employees as industrial athletes and use an outcomes-based approach proven to return them to work and life faster and more affordably."[133] Treating me for an extended period of time past my injury date would have sullied their metrics. Concentra is not unique in this regard; more than a third of over 1,000 occupational health practitioners surveyed by the Government Accountability Office reported being pressured to undertreat injured workers.[134]

In March of 2017, I started physical therapy for my back. I had planned to pay for it with private insurance because my workers' compensation claim hadn't been accepted yet when I scheduled my first session. But luckily, the clinic I chose accepted federal workers' comp, and just days before my appointment, I received an email from OWCP assigning me a case number and instructing me to share it with medical providers so they could bill OWCP. I have to say, it was nice getting in and out without a copay. I just showed up at the clinic and handed the receptionist a Form CA-17 signed by my supervisor, describing how much stooping, squatting, bending, twisting, and so forth he needed from me. The receptionist picked up a phone, dialed a number, and read off my case number. When she hung up, she said I was approved for twelve sessions.

The FECA Procedure Manual states that physical therapy is preauthorized during the first 120 days after a traumatic injury, and it further recommends that OWCP claims staff authorize therapy for a period of 60 days after an orthopedic surgery.[135] Assuming therapy begins immediately after an injury is sustained and is received three times a week, the 120 calendar days of coverage pre-approved by OWCP would allow time for 51 visits. If started immediately after surgery, the 60 calendar days of coverage customarily approved would allow time for 25 visits. In comparison, my private insurance allows 50 visits per calendar year to a physical therapist, without regard to timing relative to injury or surgery. Of course, there's a copay.

The timeframe theme is pervasive in workers' compensation, reflecting an unapologetic obsession with getting beneficiaries back to their jobs—or any other work they can perform—as hastily as possible. Not only does this cut down on the amount of time the employee is paid for doing nothing, but it also mitigates damage to the employer's experience rating and premiums. Ohio BWC preauthorizes physical therapy for only 60 days following the date of injury, and in its medical guide repeatedly admonishes its Health Partnership Program doctors to never lose sight of return-to-work goals:

> Studies have shown the likelihood of injured workers
> returning to work after six months is 50 percent. This

figure drops to 25 percent after one year and almost zero after two years on the job....[136]

As a critical player in the HPP design, providers must understand the basis and goals of return-to-work strategies and optimal return-to-work expectations for injured workers....[137]

One of the things that set HPP apart from traditional managed-care programs is the emphasis on return to work.[138]

Similarly, OWCP's Field Nurse Handbook reminds nurses to consider the following when developing case management plans:

FECA is a workers' compensation program focused on [Return to Work] efforts and is not a medical insurance or retirement plan. All efforts should focus on recovery from the accepted work-related injury and establishing work tolerance limitations as soon as medically feasible with the anticipation of ultimately obtaining a release to the full duties of the [injured worker's] date of injury job.[139]

I pay a lot of money for coverage under an employer-sponsored group health insurance policy that guarantees me a generous, well-defined level of care, with a huge provider network and a 1-800 number I can call any time, day or night, for assistance. For my back injury, I can't use that plan—not because I committed a crime or lapsed on my premiums, but because I was at work when I got hurt. Instead of my health care plan, I must use a "return-to-work" plan that guarantees me nothing and, for all I know, consults a Magic 8 Ball before responding to my doctor's treatment authorization requests. The plan has alarmingly few providers and abysmal customer support. If my treatment request is denied, all I can do about it is pay the bill myself or embark on a lengthy, possibly expensive appeal process in which the odds are stacked against me. I have no choice but to continue using that plan indefinitely, like it or not.

In an ideal free market, the offeror of a product or service is free to set his own price, and the customer/ consumer is free to not purchase the product or service at all or to purchase it from another offeror. In this way, an optimal balance is achieved between cost and quality. In a monopoly, a product or service has only one offeror or group of collaborating offerors; this arrangement leads to unreasonably high prices. The workers' compensation system is an example of another type of free market infraction – one in which the paying customer (employers) and the consumer (injured workers) are two separate entities. Instead of driving the price of medical care unfairly high, this arrangement drives quality unfairly low.

Federal lawmakers have so far refused to define a fair standard for workers' compensation medical benefits. Employers and insurers certainly wouldn't like to see that happen, so they tirelessly promote the notion that the best interests of injured workers are automatically represented by virtue of their being indistinguishable from those of their employers. Of course, that's nonsense. Employers care mostly about the *cost* of benefits; employees care about the *quality*. Employers and insurers prevail because they play the workers' compensation game with real money; injured workers bring nothing to the table except the abstract, uncountable savings their employers amass from immunity to lawsuits—a contribution that has long since been pushed from the public consciousness, taken for granted and forgotten.

"The workers compensation insurance industry and the employers who contract with them are trying to boost their profits – that is what their job is. Unfortunately, the way they are able to do it is by minimizing how much they pay out, and the way you minimize what you pay out is by curtailing the benefits. If this were just some sort of trade-off, like a business transactions, that would be one thing. But the problem is that a worker's fundamental right to get healthcare and a basic level of support they need to continue living is under impact."[140]

-Ben Palmquist, National Economic & Social Rights Initiative

CHAPTER 13

I can't believe I signed that

Before my first session of physical therapy, I was given all the usual paperwork to fill out, asking for my contact information, health history, reason for seeking care, etc. I was also given a special form just for workers' compensation patients. This form was a waiver I had to sign, acknowledging that if my physical therapist found out I had a mental illness, sexually transmitted disease, HIV, alcohol or drug addiction, or health risk based on genetic testing, he or she would likely tell my case worker, who in turn might share the information with my immediate supervisor. Now, just for the record, none of those issues apply to me, but so what if they did? It seems cruel to make a person risk disclosure of her most private and sensitive information to her employer in exchange for needed medical care.

It's understandable that workers' compensation administrators *want* that sort of information; it might help them deny a claim. For instance, what if I told my physical therapist I get drunk every morning before leaving for work? I don't, of course; but if I did, that might suggest another reason besides an icy parking lot for my accident, and workers' comp doesn't cover injuries that are caused by intoxication. Still, the fact that even genetic test results are apparently viewed as fair game goes to show there is no reasonable limit to how much prying some administrators will do, given the opportunity. What's even more disturbing is the fact that collectively they have enough political clout to stop lawmakers from *imposing* reasonable limits.

A case in point is the Genetic Information Nondiscrimination Act of 2008, which prevents employers or group health insurers from seeking genetic test data on individuals and using it in a discriminatory manner such as to influence hiring decisions or premium rates; but the Act makes a point of declaring that those protections can be overridden and ignored by any state or federal workers' compensation law.[141] Verbiage within the Act explains that it came into being because "the American public and the medical community find the existing patchwork of State and Federal laws to be confusing and inadequate to protect them from discrimination."[142] Yet the lawmakers who wrote those words took no pity on injured workers and condemned them to go on relying on an inadequate patchwork of privacy protections within an already inadequate patchwork of state and federal workers' compensation laws.

Workers' compensation benefit providers defend their turf tenaciously against privacy laws because there is potentially a lot of monetary value in an injured workers' health history. OWCP instructs its staff to collect and report it if they can. The FECA Procedure Manual advises:

> A medical opinion that takes into account the claimant's medical history, the relevant family medical history, non-work factors that could have led to the injury or disease, and a complete and consistent history of the incident or exposure or work factors alleged to be the cause of the injury or disease carries more weight than an opinion that has omissions, errors or inconsistencies in any of these areas.[143]

Similarly, field nurses are instructed to "communicate promptly to the [claims examiner] **all** case milestones/ activities that require his/her attention (i.e. work stoppage, recurrence of symptoms, unrelated medical issues)."[144]

Here's another thing that caught my eye in the Field Nurse Handbook:

> When an injured worker signs Form CA-1, Notice of Traumatic Injury, or Form CA-2, Notice of Occupational Disease, when filing a claim for workers' compensation benefits, s/he has given consent for authorization of the release of information. The Forms specifically state "I hereby authorize any physician or hospital (or any other person, institution, corporation, or government agency) to furnish any desired information to the U.S. Department of Labor, Office of Workers' Compensation Programs (or to its official representative). This authorization also permits any official representative of the Office to examine and to copy any records concerning me." As such, no additional Release of Medical Information form is necessary.[145]

I read the paragraph above in the Field Nurse Handbook and thought, *there's no way I would have signed that!* But I took a closer look at the CA-1 form I had submitted, and sure enough, there it was: a no-holds-barred privacy release. I hadn't read all the fine print before signing—though in all fairness even if I had, my only options would still have been: (1) Sign the waiver; or (2) Decline workers' comp benefits and hope my group health insurer didn't find out my injury was work-related and refuse to pay my medical bills.

Patrice Woeppel recounts in *Depraved Indifference* that after she finally managed to get workers' compensation to approve and pay for some of the medical care she needed—that is, as soon as she started costing them money—her employer began aggressively digging for dirt on her with periodic depositions:

> These lengthy inquisitions asked for everything: my birth certificate, copies of my passport, my license, my social security card; 10 years of medical history including names of all treating physicians, hospitals; household income, household expenses; income tax returns, convictions (there aren't any) and much more. These

were really fishing expeditions to see if there was anything they could possibly use, or some way they could
discredit either my claim for injury or myself.[146]

Granted, workers' compensation administrators can't reasonably
be kept in the dark about a claimant's medical condition and treatment plan, nor should they have to rely entirely on the word of the
claimant. At the same time, the fact that certain people need certain
information is not a valid excuse for opening the floodgates and
spilling a claimant's lifetime of medical history and other personal
information onto the floor for employers and insurers to pick
through looking for ammunition.

CHAPTER 14

A dirty little secret about the HIPAA Privacy Rule

The Department of Health and Human Services excluded worker's compensation claimants from medical privacy rights conferred on all other Americans under the HIPAA Privacy Rule.

The Health Insurance Portability and Accountability Act (HIPAA) was passed by Congress in 1996 to improve the efficiency and effectiveness of the health care system, particularly by making medical records portable among health care providers and insurers. HIPAA gave the Department of Health and Human Services (HHS) responsibility for choosing uniform national standards for the electronic storage, security, and transmittal of health care information. Then, recognizing the potential for electronic health care transactions to compromise a patient's privacy, HIPAA directed HHS to issue privacy regulations for those records. HHS did so by creating "The Standards for Privacy of Individually Identifiable Health Information," commonly referred to as the "Privacy Rule," which became effective in 2003.

The Privacy Rule protects all data files that include personal identifiers such as name, address, birth date, or social security number, and that relate to the individual's past, present or future physical or mental health status, health care, or payments for health care. Such information is called "protected health information (PHI)." The Privacy Rule applies to health care providers, health insurers, and health care clearinghouses (processing centers that facilitate the exchange of information between providers and insurers). These are all referred to as "covered entities." Covered entities and business associates of covered entities are permitted to use and disclose PHI without the consent of the individual to whom it pertains only for treatment, payment, and health care operations. Patients also have a right to access their own health data created, stored, or maintained by their health care providers, and to amend it if it is found to be incorrect.

HHS explains on its website what it hoped to accomplish:

> A major goal of the Privacy Rule is to assure that individuals' health information is properly protected while allowing the flow of health information needed to provide and promote high quality health care and to protect the public's health and well-being. The Rule strikes a balance that permits important uses of information, while protecting the privacy of people who seek care and healing. Given that the health care marketplace is diverse, the Rule is designed to be flexible and comprehensive to cover the variety of uses and disclosures that need to be addressed.[147]

We have all signed HIPAA forms at a doctor's office. It's not the doctor's idea to have us do this. The HIPAA Privacy Rule grants individuals "a right to adequate notice of the uses and disclosures of protected health information that may be made by the covered entity, and of the individual's rights and the covered entity's legal duties with respect to protected health information."[148] This purpose is typically served by a HIPAA Release form, which in addition to providing notification, also requests the names of individuals (such as family members or caretakers) to whom the patient authorizes disclosure of his or her PHI.

The detailed workings of the HIPAA Privacy Rule are spelled out in the Code of Federal Regulations Title 45, Parts 160 and 164. Workers' compensation is mentioned only in Section 164.512, which describes special circumstances in which a covered entity sometimes *may* legally disclose PHI without first attempting to notify or obtain consent from the individual to whom it pertains. In addition to workers' compensation purposes, those circumstances include disclosures made for such purposes as reporting abuse, neglect, or crime; or to protect public health or inform an individual that he or she may be at risk of contracting a disease; or in response to a court order; or for national security purposes; or for research purposes that are shown to pose minimal risk to the privacy of individuals. A limited set of descriptive PHI may be disclosed for the purpose of locating a suspect, witness, or missing person.

Disclosure of a prison inmate's PHI is permitted to some extent, to facilitate health care for that inmate and to protect other inmates and prison staff. Below is the unabridged wording of that exemption.

45 CFR 164.512 (k)(5) *Correctional institutions and other law enforcement custodial situations* —

(i) *Permitted disclosures.* A covered entity may disclose to a correctional institution or a law enforcement official having lawful custody of an inmate or other individual protected health information about such inmate or individual, if the correctional institution or such law enforcement official represents that such protected health information is necessary for:

(A) The provision of health care to such individuals;

(B) The health and safety of such individual or other inmates;

(C) The health and safety of the officers or employees of or others at the correctional institution;

(D) The health and safety of such individuals and officers or other persons responsible for the transporting of inmates or their transfer from one institution, facility, or setting to another;

(E) Law enforcement on the premises of the correctional institution; or

(F) The administration and maintenance of the safety, security, and good order of the correctional institution.

(ii) *Permitted uses.* A covered entity that is a correctional institution may use protected health information of individuals who are inmates for any purpose for which such protected health information may be disclosed.

(iii) *No application after release.* For the purposes of this provision, an individual is no longer an inmate when released on parole, probation, supervised release, or otherwise is no longer in lawful custody.

Compare the exemption above, for criminals, to the one below, for workers' compensation claimants:

45 CFR 164.512 (l) *Standard: disclosures for workers' compensation.* A covered entity may disclose protected health information as authorized by and to the extent necessary to comply with laws relating to workers' compensation or other similar programs, established by law, that provide benefits for work-related injuries or illness without regard to fault.

That's the whole thing. Notice how much less robust the privacy protections are for injured workers than for incarcerated criminals. In fact, the HIPAA Privacy Rule doesn't impose *any* limitations whatsoever of its own on workers' compensation-related disclosures. It simply throws claimants over the fence to whichever federal or state workers' comp law might apply, without any apparent regard for what sorts of privacy protections, if any, await them there. An analogous approach to incarcerated criminals would be to authorize any disclosure of their PHI that conforms with whatever policies happen to be in place at the prisons to which they are sent.

In all fairness to HHS, the 1996 HIPAA law enacted by Congress, which gave HHS its marching orders to adopt and enforce uniform national standards for organization and transmittal of electronic medical records, declared that workers' compensation records were not to be included.[149] But while workers' comp entities were clearly meant to be exempted from the HIPAA standards pertaining to uniformity and portability of medical records, it's less obvious what standards they should be held to for privacy protection. Fortunately, Congress established the National Committee on Vital and Health Statistics (NCVHS) in 1949 to advise the HHS Secretary on any and all matters related to information policy. On the topic of workers' compensation disclosures under the Privacy Rule, the NCVHS weighed in as follows:

> Workers compensation is a complex subject that requires special treatment and reasonable accommodation. However, like other casualty insurance, it is not entitled to a complete exemption. The Department should not evade its responsibility to address these difficult issues by simply exempting them. If necessary, a separate and subsequent rulemaking should consider how to meet confidentiality interests of patients while allowing workers' compensation to be administered efficiently.[150]

The draft Privacy Rule published by HHS in the Federal Register on November 3, 1999 proposed a general paragraph that would govern disclosures for purposes mandated by any other laws. For workers' compensation purposes in particular, covered entities would be permitted to disclose protected health information "to an insurer or employer for the purposes of determining an individual's eligibility for medical or other benefits, or for the purpose of determining fitness for duty."[151] When making disclosures to a non-covered entity, health care providers would be bound by all applicable requirements of the Privacy Rule unless the other law (e.g., a workers' compensation law) contained provisions that were contrary to provisions of the Privacy Rule "and more protective of the individual's privacy."[152] The Federal Register notice of this proposed law gave the public until January 3, 2000 to submit comments.

Much had changed by the time HHS published its final version of the Privacy Rule in the Federal Register on December 28, 2000. Workers' compensation now had a paragraph all to itself, with wording that permitted not just disclosures that are *mandated by* other laws, but *as authorized by* workers' compensation laws in particular. This new paragraph, 45 CFR 164.512(l), gives workers' compensation lawmakers unchecked power to authorize disclosures of health information; it is generally construed as a full waiver of medical privacy rights for claimants.[153] HHS rationalized, "Our review of state workers' compensation laws suggests that many of these laws address the issue of the scope of information that is available to carriers and employers."[154] Apparently, HHS decided that all the medical privacy any injured worker needs is the knowledge that "many" state workers' comp laws "address the issue" in some manner. HHS also absurdly advised that a claimant's right to privacy should be renegotiated on a case-by-case basis in a series of friendly conversations: "Where the law is silent, the workers' compensation carrier and covered health care provider will need to discuss what information is necessary for the carrier to administer the claim, and the health care provider may disclose that information."[155]

In a Federal Register paragraph titled "Additional Considerations," HHS did finally acknowledge the gaping hole in its Privacy Rule:

> We have included a general authorization for disclosures under workers' compensation systems to be consistent with the intent of Congress, which defined workers' compensation carriers as excepted benefits under HIPAA. We recognize that there are significant privacy issues raised by how individually identifiable health information is used and disclosed in workers' compensation systems, and believe that states or the

federal government should enact standards that address those concerns."[156]

Decades later, no such standards have been enacted by the federal government, nor by most states.[157] HHS currently meanders aimlessly around the subject in an article on its website:

Disclosures for Workers' Compensation Purposes[158]
[45 CFR 164.512(l)]

Background

The HIPAA Privacy Rule does not apply to entities that are either workers' compensation insurers, workers' compensation administrative agencies, or employers, except to the extent they may otherwise be covered entities. However, these entities need access to the health information of individuals who are injured on the job or who have a work-related disease to process or adjudicate claims, or to coordinate care under workers' compensation systems. Generally, this health information is obtained from health care providers who treat these individuals and who may be covered by the Privacy Rule. The Privacy Rule recognizes the legitimate need of insurers and other entities involved in the workers' compensation systems to have access to individuals' health information as authorized by State or other law. Due to the significant variability among such laws, the Privacy Rule permits disclosures of health information for workers' compensation purposes in a number of different ways.

It's all well and good for HHS to recognize "the legitimate need of insurers and other entities involved in the workers' compensation system to have access to individuals' health information," but what happened to its original Privacy Rule goal of striking "a balance that permits important uses of information, while protecting the privacy of people who seek care and healing"?

Further into the article, HHS tries to mollify its website visitors with a "Minimum Necessary" standard, copied below, that isn't actually in the law. Its first three sentences form a classic shit sandwich—the first and third seem promising, but the middle sentence steals the promise back with: "Under this requirement, protected health information may be shared for such purposes to the full extent authorized by State or other law." And here we are back where we started, with HIPAA relinquishing nothing to injured workers.

> Minimum Necessary. Covered entities are required reasonably to limit the amount of protected health information disclosed under 45 CFR 164.512(l) to the minimum necessary to accomplish the workers' compensation purpose. Under this requirement, protected health information may be shared for such purposes to the full extent authorized by State or other law. In addition, covered entities are required reasonably to limit the amount of protected health information disclosed for payment purposes to the minimum necessary.

The two paragraphs that follow the one above are nothing but fluff—a string of permission statements (e.g., **are permitted to, may, are not required to**) rather than requirement statements (e.g., **are required to, must, may not**). I changed the font to bold where those types of words appear, to make the pattern more apparent.

> Covered entities **are permitted to** disclose the amount and types of protected health information that are necessary to obtain payment for health care provided to an injured or ill worker. Where a covered entity routinely makes disclosures for workers' compensation purposes under 45 CFR 164.512(l) or for payment purposes, the covered entity **may** develop standard protocols as part of its minimum necessary policies and procedures that

address the type and amount of protected health information to be disclosed for such purposes.

Where protected health information is requested by a State workers' compensation or other public official, covered entities **are permitted to** reasonably rely on the official's representations that the information requested is the minimum necessary for the intended purpose. See 45 CFR 164.514(d)(3)(iii)(A). Covered entities **are not required to** make a minimum necessary determination when disclosing protected health information as required by State or other law, or pursuant to the individual's authorization. See 45 CFR 164.502(b).

The so-called "Minimum Necessary" standard above is the very opposite of what it pretends to be. Not only does it impose no actual limits or requirements on covered entities, but it effectively tells them they needn't worry about how much of a patient's protected health information could possibly be relevant to the workers' compensation purpose and can instead go ahead and hand over everything an administrator asks them for without fear of legal reprisal.

Now, bear with me, but there really *is* a Minimum Necessary clause in the HIPAA Privacy Rule, codified in 45 CFR 164.502(b)—but it's not the one you just read. Below is the *real*, statutory version of the Minimum Necessary standard, which applies to everyone *except* injured workers:

45 CFR 164.502 (b) Standard: Minimum necessary— Minimum necessary applies. When using or disclosing protected health information or when requesting protected health information from another covered entity or business associate, a covered entity or business associate must make reasonable efforts to limit protected health information to the minimum necessary to accomplish the intended purpose of the use, disclosure, or request.

And below is the extensive CFR section that defines what is required of covered entities in order to comply with the *real* Minimum Necessary rule above. Again, I'm using bold font to call attention to all the words that introduce requirement or permission statements.

45 CFR 164.514 Other requirements relating to uses and disclosures of protected health information.

(d)(1) Standard: minimum necessary requirements. In order to comply with §164.502(b) and this section, a covered entity **must** meet the requirements of paragraphs (d)(2) through (d)(5) of this section with respect to a request for, or the use and disclosure of, protected health information.

(2) Implementation specifications: Minimum necessary uses of protected health information. (i) A covered entity **must** identify:

(A) Those persons or classes of persons, as appropriate, in its workforce who need access to protected health information to carry out their duties; and

(B) For each such person or class of persons, the category or categories of protected health information to which access is needed and any conditions appropriate to such access.

(ii) A covered entity **must** make reasonable efforts to limit the access of such persons or classes identified in paragraph (d)(2)(i)(A) of this section to protected health information consistent with paragraph (d)(2)(i)(B) of this section.

(3) Implementation specification: Minimum necessary disclosures of protected health information. (i) For any type of disclosure that it makes on a routine and recurring basis, a covered entity **must** implement policies and procedures (which **may be** standard protocols)

that limit the protected health information disclosed to the amount reasonably necessary to achieve the purpose of the disclosure.

(ii) For all other disclosures, a covered entity **must**:

(A) Develop criteria designed to limit the protected health information disclosed to the information reasonably necessary to accomplish the purpose for which disclosure is sought; and

(B) Review requests for disclosure on an individual basis in accordance with such criteria.

(iii) A covered entity **may** rely, if such reliance is reasonable under the circumstances, on a requested disclosure as the minimum necessary for the stated purpose when:

(A) Making disclosures to public officials that are permitted under §164.512, if the public official represents that the information requested is the minimum necessary for the stated purpose(s);

(B) The information is requested by another covered entity;

(C) The information is requested by a professional who is a member of its workforce or is a business associate of the covered entity for the purpose of providing professional services to the covered entity, if the professional represents that the information requested is the minimum necessary for the stated purpose(s); or

(D) Documentation or representations that comply with the applicable requirements of §164.512(i) have been provided by a person requesting the information for research purposes.

(4) Implementation specifications: Minimum necessary requests for protected health information. (i) A covered entity **must** limit any request for protected health

information to that which is reasonably necessary to accomplish the purpose for which the request is made, when requesting such information from other covered entities.

(ii) For a request that is made on a routine and recurring basis, a covered entity **must** implement policies and procedures (which **may be** standard protocols) that limit the protected health information requested to the amount reasonably necessary to accomplish the purpose for which the request is made.

(iii) For all other requests, a covered entity **must**:

(A) Develop criteria designed to limit the request for protected health information to the information reasonably necessary to accomplish the purpose for which the request is made; and

(B) Review requests for disclosure on an individual basis in accordance with such criteria.

(5) Implementation specification: Other content requirement. For all uses, disclosures, or requests to which the requirements in paragraph (d) of this section apply, a covered entity **may not** use, disclose or request an entire medical record, except when the entire medical record is specifically justified as the amount that is reasonably necessary to accomplish the purpose of the use, disclosure, or request.

Evidently, in crafting their pretend version of the Minimum Necessary standard for workers' compensation disclosures, our friends and protectors in HHS methodically picked through the *real* Minimum Necessary standard for permission statements only, leaving out each and every actual requirement that might cramp the style of workers' comp administrators. After finding a way to confer privacy protections on every other group of Americans, including prisoners and fugitives, HHS sold injured workers out. It's not that injured workers are on a lower rung of the social ladder than serial killers; it's just that their medical history, in all its glorious detail, is a valuable commodity that can sometimes help administrators deny claims and requests for medical treatment, saving themselves money. There is doubtless a lot of pressure on lawmakers to grant them unfettered access.

Hypocritically, HHS waxed poetic in the November 3, 1999 Federal Register about the sacredness of individual privacy and its transcendence over economic considerations:

> Privacy is a fundamental right. As such, it has to be viewed differently than any ordinary economic good. Although the costs and benefits of a regulation need to be considered as a means of identifying and weighing options, it is important not to lose sight of the inherent meaning of privacy: it speaks to our individual and collective freedom.[159]

Even if HHS had done a credible job of protecting the privacy of injured workers, the following frequently asked question on its website makes a painfully valid point:

> FAQ[160]:
> My state law says I may provide information regarding an injured workers' [sic] previous condition, which is not directly related to the claim for compensation, to an employer or insurer if I obtain the workers'[sic] written release. Am I permitted to make this disclosure under the HIPAA Privacy Rule?

> Answer:
> A covered entity may disclose protected health information where the individual's written authorization has been obtained, consistent with the Privacy Rule's requirements at 45 CFR 164.508. Thus, a covered entity would be permitted to make the above disclosure if the individual signed such an authorization.

For people such as myself who had to sign a draconian privacy release to apply for workers' compensation benefits, the confiscation of our HIPAA privacy rights pretty much amounts to beating a dead horse. Still, it seems to me that there ought to at least be clear notification when those rights are signed away, so applicants understand what they're giving up (I sure didn't). Isn't it odd that HIPAA law requires every doctor who respects your privacy rights to remind you about them, but allows a workers' comp entity to revoke them without warning? The Privacy Rule prohibits the practice of requiring anyone else to sign the sort of blanket waiver many workers' comp claimants must sign, because "When an individual is required to sign a blanket authorization at the point of receiving care or enrolling for coverage, that consent is often not voluntary because the individual must sign the form as a condition of treatment or payment for treatment."[161] Why wouldn't this argument apply to workers' comp claimants? Why is their forced "consent" considered valid?

In response to enactment of the HIPAA Privacy Rule, OWCP published an open letter online to medical providers, proactively straightening out any confusion they might have regarding their obligation to their patients.[162] The letter advised that providers should continue to share information and documentation as they always had with OWCP, explaining that:

> Although OWCP is not covered by the HIPAA regulations (because it is neither a health care provider nor a "covered entity" within the definitions of the rule), OWCP is committed to preserving the privacy of claimants' medical information, as required by the Privacy Act. Under that statute privacy protected information disclosures are strictly limited, and violations of the Act are punishable by criminal penalties. OWCP may disclose health care or other information contained in a system of records maintained under unique individual identifiers, such as OWCP case files, only upon either the written authorization of the claimant, a court order,

or a properly promulgated routine use. Only authorized federal employees or contractors have access to medical records information. In addition, all OWCP contractors with access to such information have written contract provisions that require them to comply with the Privacy Act. Therefore, OWCP only discloses sensitive health care information to those permitted to receive such information under the Privacy Act, and only for purposes directly related to the mission of the agency.

OWCP's letter urges us not to fret about losing out on the HIPAA Privacy Rule. Who needs it, anyway, when we've got the Privacy Act?

CHAPTER 15

A dirty little secret about the Privacy Act

OWCP is exempt from honoring many of the Privacy Act protections because it categorizes all of its workers' compensation files as criminal investigation files.

The HIPAA Privacy Rule and the Privacy Act have similar sounding names, but they are different laws. As discussed in the previous chapter, the HIPAA Privacy Rule protects health information by telling covered entities (health care providers, health insurers, and health care clearinghouses) what types of patient information must be protected and to whom and under what circumstances it may be disclosed. The Privacy Act of 1974 (5 U.S.C. 552a "Records maintained on individuals") governs the collection, maintenance, use, and dissemination of any information about individuals that is stored in systems of records by federal agencies. States have their own versions of the Privacy Act, which apply to state agencies. A system of records is any group of records under the control of an agency, from which information is retrieved by the name of the individual or by some unique identifier assigned to the individual, such as social security number. What the HIPAA Privacy Rule and the Privacy Act of 1974 have in common is a goal of balancing the need to maintain information about individuals with the individuals' right to privacy.

The federal Privacy Act covers more types of stored data than does the Privacy Rule (which applies only to medical records), but the Act is far less restrictive in that it allows agencies to decide for themselves what information they will collect and how they will use or disclose it, as long as they first publish all the following information in the Federal Register: the name and storage location of the system; the types of records it contains; the categories of individuals on whom those records are maintained; all potential sources of information; each routine use for the records; and the applicable policies and practices regarding storage, retrievability, access, retention, and disposal of the records. The agency must also publish procedures whereby an individual can be notified at his request if the system contains a record pertaining to him, and procedures whereby he can gain access to it and contest its content. The point of providing such detailed advance notice in the Federal Register is so that issues can be raised and resolved before the system of records is put into effect. However, while the public may provide feedback or ask for clarification, it cannot reject any aspect of a new or changing system of records.

DOL/GOVT-1 is the name of the Privacy Act system that contains all FECA case files owned and managed by OWCP. Below is the list of every kind of record DOL/GOVT-1 may contain. I have used bold font to highlight a catch-all phrase that effectively declares nothing off-limits, and another phrase that makes every OWCP case file a potential criminal investigation file; the significance of that will be apparent soon.

> Reports of injury by the employee and/or employing agency; claim forms filed by or on behalf of injured Federal employees or their survivors seeking benefits under FECA; forms authorizing medical care and treatment; other medical records and reports; bills and other payment records; compensation payment records; formal orders for or against the payment of benefits; transcripts of hearings conducted; and **any other medical, employment, or personal information submitted or**

gathered in connection with the claim. The system may also contain information relating to dates of birth, marriage, divorce, and death; notes of telephone conversations conducted in connection with the claim; information relating to vocational and/or medical rehabilitation plans and progress reports; records relating to court proceedings, insurance, banking and employment; articles from newspapers and other publications; information relating to other benefits (financial and otherwise) the claimant may be entitled to; and **information received from various investigative agencies concerning possible violations of Federal civil or criminal law**. The system may also contain information relating to certain claims under the War Hazards Compensation Act (WHCA). The system may also contain consumer credit reports on individuals indebted to the United States, information relating to the debtor's assets, liabilities, income and expenses, personal financial statements, correspondence to and from the debtor, information relating to the location of the debtor, and other records and reports relating to the implementation of the Federal Claims Collection Act (as amended), including investigative reports or administrative review matters.[163]

The Privacy Act prohibits the disclosure of data from an individual's record without the written consent of the individual; however, there are 12 exceptions to that rule, most of them fairly benign. For instance, data from any system of records may be disclosed to employees of the agency which maintains the record, if they have a need to know; or to the Census Bureau, as relevant for planning or carrying out a census; or for use in statistical research, if transferred in a form that is not individually identifiable. Data may also be disclosed for a "routine use," which is literally any use that has been declared in the Federal Register. The Department of Labor currently claims 14 *universal* routine uses for every system of records it maintains, and OWCP claims 21 *specific* routine uses for the DOL/GOVT-1 system, some of which overlap with the Department's universal routine uses.

The Department of Labor's complete list of 14 universal routine uses can be found on its website.[164] I'll show just one of them here, Number 6, because it's general enough to make the others more or less moot. In essence, anyone hired or requested by the Department to do anything at all for it can be given any of the information in any of its files. A note is tacked onto this sweeping routine use in an apparent attempt to maintain control of information after it's been released, by making a circular reference back to the Privacy Act.

> 6. To disclose to contractors, employees of contractors, consultants, grantees, and volunteers who have been engaged to assist the agency in the performance of or working on a contract, service, grant, cooperative agreement or other activity or service for the Federal Government.
>
> Note: Recipients shall be required to comply with the requirements of the Privacy Act of 1974, as amended, 5 U.S.C. 552a; see also 5 U.S.C. 552a(m).

The Department of Labor's website also lists all 21 of OWCP's *specific* routine uses for the DOL/GOVT-1 system of records, designated by the letters a through u.[165] Again, I'll just show the obligatory catch-all category here, buried in the middle at the 11th position, letter k:

> k. To contractors providing services to the Department or any other Federal agency or any other individual or entity specified in any of these routine uses or in the Department's General Prefatory Statement who require the data to perform the services that they have contracted to perform, provided that those services are consistent with the routine use for which the information was disclosed to the contracting entity. Should

such a disclosure be made to the contractor, the individual or entity making such disclosure shall ensure that the contractor complies fully with all Privacy Act provisions, including those prohibiting unlawful disclosure of such information.

The Privacy Act is flexible to a fault; nevertheless, OWCP touts its allegiance to the Act and plays up its value to FECA claimants. Benefit application forms CA-1 and CA-2 include a Privacy Act disclosure on the back side that lists some, though not all, of the routine uses declared for DOL/GOVT-1. The Privacy Act also gets a shout-out in FECA administrative law:

20 CFR 10.10 Are all documents relating to claims filed under the FECA considered confidential?

All records relating to claims for benefits, including copies of such records maintained by an employer, are considered confidential and may not be released, inspected, copied or otherwise disclosed except as provided in the Freedom of Information Act and the Privacy Act of 1974 or under the routine uses provided by DOL/GOVT-1 if such release is consistent with the purpose for which the record was created.

The Privacy Act isn't *all* about controlling disclosure of records. It imposes other restrictions as well. For instance, a record may contain only such information about an individual as is "relevant and necessary" to accomplish a legally authorized purpose, and to the greatest extent practicable, the information is to be collected directly from the subject to whom it pertains. Records that are used to make any determination about an individual must be maintained with "such accuracy, relevance, timeliness, and completeness as is reasonably necessary to assure fairness to the individual." Appropriate safeguards must be established to ensure the security and confidentiality of records.[166]

Each agency is required to establish rules and procedures for notifying an individual, in response to his request, if a particular system of records contains a record pertaining to him. It must define reasonable times, places, and requirements for disclosing an individual's record to him after verifying his identify. An individual must be permitted to obtain a copy of his own record, and to request an amendment of it. An agency is not required to make every requested amendment; but when it decides not to do so, it must allow the individual to append his record with a statement expressing disagreement. Each agency is required to keep a list of all disclosures made of each record and allow the individual named in the record to see that list. The agency must notify everyone to whom the record has been disclosed when there are any subsequent corrections or disputes.

In principle, that all sounds pretty good; in practice, there's a catch. While the Privacy Act itself is codified in 5 U.S.C. 552a, the Department of Labor's internal regulations for *implementing* the Act are found in 29 CFR Part 71 "Protection of Individual Privacy and Access to Records under the Privacy Act of 1974." In Section 71.51, the Department lists 39 systems of records for which it claims exemption from many Privacy Act rules because those records "contain investigatory material compiled for law enforcement purposes." Number one on the list is *DOL/GOVT-1 (Office of Workers' Compensation Programs, Federal Employees' Compensation Act File)*. Recall that one type of information preapproved for inclusion in DOL/GOVT-1 records is "information received from various investigative agencies concerning possible violations of Federal civil or criminal law." As it turns out, a file that even *may* contain criminal investigation material gets special treatment under the Privacy Act, earning protection not just *for* but also *from* the individual to whom it pertains.

Only specific Privacy Act rules are waived for DOL/GOVT-1 and the other 38 exempted Department of Labor systems, but they comprise a significant subset of the Privacy Act protections. In brief, here is what those waivers mean to a FECA claimant: OWCP staff can collect as much information on you as they like, and it does not have to be relevant in any way to your workers' compensation claim. They don't have to show you what's in your file or even tell you that they have a file on you if you ask. They don't have to tell you where they got the information in your file. They don't have to tell you who else has seen it. The only caveat is that if they deny a claim based on specific information in your file, they have to share that information with you on request, unless doing so would reveal the identity of a source who provided the information on the condition of anonymity.

Of course, the fact that OWCP doesn't *have* to do those things doesn't necessarily mean it *never* does them. According to the Federal Register notice for the DOL/GOVT-1 system of records, OWCP singles out only certain materials in a case file for exemption from Privacy Act rules; specifically, any dirt ("investigative material," that is) it collects or tries to collect on the claimant.[167] The rest is presumably accessible to him or her. OWCP has a procedure by which claimants can obtain a copy of their records, but based on my experience, it's an incomplete copy, with no mention of what's missing. The next chapter goes into more detail on that.

CHAPTER 16

Information spills

A week into physical therapy, I received a letter from OWCP that began like this:

> Dear Ms. HICKS:
>
> When your claim was received, it appeared to be a minor injury that resulted in minimal or no lost time from work. Based on these criteria, and because your employing agency did not controvert Continuation of Pay (COP) or challenge the merits of the case, payment of a limited amount of medical expenses was administratively approved. The merits of the claim, however, have not been formally considered.
>
> Your claim has now been reopened for consideration because the medical bills have exceeded $1500.

My initial reaction was surprise at learning that OWCP viewed my broken back as "a minor injury that resulted in minimal or no lost time from work" and that my employing agency had not controverted my COP after all. But my confusion was cleared up further into the letter, where it became apparent that OWCP was referencing an injury that had occurred at a different Air Force base from mine; one I had never visited. Under the mistaken impression that I was injured in another state and must therefore have been on travel status that day, OWCP asked me in the letter to have my supervisor submit a statement to that effect, and also wanted to know, "When the accident occurred, were you on the most direct route between the point of last official duty and next expected official duty?" I contacted my case worker and claims examiner immediately, letting them know there had been a mix-up. Both responded within the week, acknowledging that someone else's case file contents had been mixed with mine by mistake and telling me to disregard the strange letter.

In April 2017, I received a letter from OWCP telling me my case had been accepted, for real this time. I had very mixed feelings about that. On the one hand, I would have thought it unfair if my case had been denied. On the other hand, I had come to appreciate insurance copays as a small price to pay for medical privacy, dignity, and easy, assured access to quality care. My claim acceptance letter stated: "Your Primary Point of Contact for any questions regarding your work-related injury is your immediate supervisor." My supervisor received a corresponding letter informing him that he was my primary point of contact for questions regarding my work injury and instructing him to contact my case worker if I had any questions he couldn't answer. My supervisor was a nice guy who I'm certain wished me well, but he knew no more about workers' compensation than I did and it made no sense for me to route my questions through him; so I emailed my case worker directly, which she assured me was fine.

There is a process by which FECA claimants can request a copy of their own case files.[168] I decided to take OWCP up on that offer for a couple of reasons. First, I wanted to be sure all my documents—and no one else's—were in there. Also, I was curious to see what else my boss had been asked besides whether or not I steal office supplies, and who else might have been asked similar questions about me. I mailed a request for my case file and received it on a DVD about a month later. It contained the letter I had sent my claims examiner informing him that some of the questions he was asking did not pertain to me; and his return letter acknowledging that he had me confused with someone else and to ignore the extraneous questions; and a written summary of telephone communications between my case worker and claims examiner, in which they concluded that my file had been conflated with the file of a man I'll refer to as Mr. X.

My case file also contained a copy of my Position Requirements Document (PRD), describing my job requirements and responsibilities; and Mr. X's PRD, describing his job requirements and responsibilities. My file contained a personnel document filled out with my social security number, date of birth, and salary; and a personnel document for Mr. X. that revealed his social security number, date of birth, and salary. It contained my MRI report, as well as examination and treatment notes from my doctor and my physical therapist. And it contained a form filled out by Mr. X's doctor, describing his injury and treatment. Mr. X, like me, had fallen on ice. He was diagnosed with a concussion, bruised scalp, and pulled muscle in his neck. Wouldn't you think he ought to have taken a day or two off work to recuperate? Mr. X's doctor filled out a workers' comp medical form clearing him to go back to work the very next morning. *Ouch.*

There was one other "bonus" document in my case file – a handwritten note from a mail carrier in which he described injuring his back while twisting around to reach into the back of his mail truck. Neither the type nor date of injury matched mine, but in OWCP's defense, his case number differs from mine by just one digit, and his handwriting isn't the best. There was no trace of my supervisor (or anyone else) being asked to evaluate my character, so I know I wasn't given all the information OWCP had collected on me.

Naturally, I emailed my case worker immediately, telling her I had been sent some of Mr. X's private information by mistake and offering to send it back. When she hadn't responded eight days later, I sent a letter to my claims examiner. Five days after dropping that letter in the mail, I finally got an email back from my case worker: "Sorry this is so late getting back to you," she wrote, "been catching up on e-mails." Regarding the information spill I had reported, she simply informed me that she had received a copy of my letter to the claims examiner and had uploaded it to my file. She also answered a question I had asked regarding how to handle a medical bill I had received, with guidance that turned out to be wrong. Then she wrote that my physical therapy provider hadn't been paid for the treatment I'd received months earlier. She advised that I contact the clinic and tell them to resubmit their bills. I balked initially, thinking surely that was her job, not mine, but I went ahead and did it anyway for the sake of my physical therapist, who I thought deserved to be paid.

Months later, I requested another copy of my case file just to verify that it had been sifted apart from everyone else's. I'm happy to say that the mail carrier's note was gone, as well as all but three pages of Mr. X's personnel document; the pages left behind contained no sensitive information, so I let it go. I wonder if anyone ever told Mr. X what happened. I looked him up in the phone directory at work once and considered contacting him, but I didn't because I thought it might just alarm him for no good reason. I'm certainly not going to steal his identity, and I hope the same would be said by any FECA claimants out there who have *my* personal information.

Wondering what OWCP's official procedure is for handling information spills, or if they even have one, I searched online and found OWCP Bulletin No. 08-01 *How to Handle Information Spills*, issued January 23, 2008. The first step an OWCP employee is instructed to follow upon discovering that one individual's personal information has been inadvertently released to another, is this: "Begin the document recapture process by asking the individual to return the document in question (either via telephone or registered mail) and offering a self-addressed, stamped envelope for return of the material directly to the district office for re-filing or destruction."[169] Not only was I not asked to return Mr. X's personal information, but OWCP actually ignored my *offer* to do so. Federal civilian employees who wish to file a workers' compensation claim must hand their personal information over to an agency that is hopelessly bad at protecting it and cannot be held accountable for its carelessness.

The Privacy Act – from which OWCP claims partial exemption—carries civil and criminal penalties for improper disclosure of protected information, though they are weak. An agency or person found guilty in court of *intentionally* disclosing personal information in a manner prohibited by the Privacy Act may be held liable for any monetary damages caused by the violation and may also be found guilty of a misdemeanor and fined up to $5,000. There are no penalties for *accidental* disclosures stemming from carelessness.[170]

The HIPAA Privacy Rule—from which OWCP enjoys total exemption—mandates that if a covered entity discovers a breach in security for protected health information, it must notify each individual whose unsecured protected health information has been, or may have been, accessed, acquired, used, or disclosed as a result of the breach. This notification must be made no later than 60 days after the breach was discovered or should have been discovered through the exercise of reasonable diligence.[171] Monetary penalties of up to $50,000 can be assessed for willful violation of HIPAA rules.[172]

CHAPTER 17

The myth that it's common for employees to fake or exaggerate injuries to collect workers' compensation

When I broke my back at work and applied for workers' compensation, I was keenly aware of the fact that I was suddenly living in the shadow of a stereotype. The stereotype I'm talking about is painted pretty well by the excerpt below from an article posted on the website of Hub International, a company that sells workers' compensation insurance policies to businesses.

> **We're All Paying the Price of Employee-perpetuated Worker's Compensation Fraud**
>
> Joe hurt his back on the job and is out on leave. Four weeks later, after a rigorous bout of physical therapy, his doctor cleared him to return to work in a modified capacity. The issue is that Joe doesn't like his job, nor does he want to return to the modified duty position. By staying home from work, is Joe malingering? Is he committing Workers' Compensation fraud?
>
> Yes. He is.
>
> Of the three types of Workers' Compensation fraud – employer, vendor and employee fraud – the latter is the most talked about, comprising 20 percent of annual WC claims paid. Employee fraud can happen in the form of

an alleged accident that never actually occurred or when an employee is injured at work and exaggerates his disability and fails to return to work when he is capable.

While it is possible that an employee might stage an accident, it is very rare and 95 percent of Workers' Comp claims involve a real accident at work. By far the largest percentage of employee Workers' Compensation fraud claims happen when an employee—like Joe—continues to claim disability and collect weekly benefits while they are in fact capable of returning to work.[173]

Many of us have seen surveillance videos on television of people who supposedly can't work because of back injuries or some similar complaint lifting heavy loads out in public. It's fun to watch shows like that; seeing cheaters get caught is gratifying. There's a public appetite for "Gotcha!" stories, and the media obliges. But the fact that so much attention is paid to workers' compensation fraud, and so little is paid to other types—such as homeowner's or car insurance fraud, for instance—creates a skewed perception of the relative frequencies of those crimes that is actually reversed from reality. Fraud has been found to account for between 13 and 17 percent of total claims payments for auto insurance bodily injury,[174] while studies consistently find that only one or two percent *at most* of workers' compensation claims involve fraud of any kind.[175] The warping of public opinion in this regard was, and still is, intentional.

Following publication of the National Commission's report on workers' compensation in 1972, states advanced toward the goal of meeting the Commission's 19 essential recommendations. Not only did this increase the average claim cost, but it also increased awareness of workers' compensation while making it a more favorable option for injured workers, thus increasing the number of claims filed and causing the dollar amount of benefits to increase by more than expected.[176] This trend was exacerbated by rapidly rising medical care costs. The spread of private health insurance throughout the mid-1900s, along with the introduction of Medicare and Medicaid in 1966, drove increases in the cost of medical care both directly through increased demand and indirectly by fostering a succession of medical breakthroughs, technology enhancements, and development of new pharmaceuticals.[177]

Heading into the 1990s, benefit costs were climbing at an unprecedented rate. Private carriers that sold workers' compensation policies to businesses were uniquely challenged by the fact that they were regulated; that is, required by state laws to provide certain benefits to claimants and to charge premiums within certain defined limits to businesses. Many withdrew from the market, while those that remained cast about for ways to become profitable again. Faced with the choice of lobbying either for higher premiums limits or lower benefit levels, naturally they gravitated toward—and had better success with—the latter.[178] Employers were the insurance carriers' customers, not to mention an organized force to be reckoned with. Lowering benefit levels was an easier sell, though not quite as easy as insurers and employers both would have liked, even with memories of the National Commission fading. A campaign to discredit and erode sympathy for injured workers began to take shape.

"It was a crisis, and the insurers needed ways to persuade the legislatures to restrict their costs. Fraud was one of the images they used to justify narrowing eligibility, changing the way you measure benefits and basically saving money for employers at the expense of injured workers."[179]
  - *Edward Welch, Director, Workers' Compensation Center at Michigan State University*

In 1989, the Alliance of American Insurers kicked off a national campaign to contain workers' compensation costs by "reforming" state laws, and also announced that it was making workers' compensation fraud a legislative priority. Shortly thereafter, more than two-thirds of the states enacted laws making insurance fraud a felony, and many states launched formal anti-fraud enforcement efforts. Video surveillance of workers' comp recipients became commonplace, and videos of supposedly disabled workers engaging in physical activities outside of work were sensationalized by the media, widely distributed, and eagerly consumed by the public. Most Americans purchase homeowner's or car insurance and anticipate at least a reasonable likelihood of having to file a claim against those policies someday, but most have no expectation of ever filing a workers' compensation claim and are therefore receptive to the idea that people who do are up to no good. Thus, vivid anecdotes of claimant fraud were impactful, though they belied the fact that very little of it was actually found. Investigators discovered that fraud committed by employers and medical care providers is more pervasive and costly by far.[180]

Workers' compensation fraud encompasses any self-serving lie or misrepresentation made by anyone, including but not limited to employers, employees, medical care providers, and insurers. Employees can commit fraud by making up an injury or disease, exaggerating symptoms, or claiming benefits for an injury that actually occurred outside of the workplace. They can also commit fraud by supplementing wage replacement benefits with unreported income. Employers can commit fraud by faking payroll data to lower their premiums or by not purchasing coverage at all, giving themselves an unfair advantage over their competitors. Employers can also commit fraud by failing to process claims submitted by injured workers. Medical care providers can commit fraud by charging for treatment that wasn't necessary or wasn't actually provided. Insurers can commit fraud by denying or delaying payment of legitimate claims.

There is consensus among those who have studied the issue of workers' compensation fraud that fraud committed by employers and medical care providers is far more common and more costly than claimant fraud, though claimant fraud receives by far the most publicity.[181] The ulterior motive of the anti-fraud campaign was becoming apparent at least to scholars by 1998, when State University of New York Professor Martha McCluskey wrote: "The immense political and media attention directed at claims fraud suggests that the purpose is not to produce significant cost savings through controlling blatant fraud, but to shift the political climate in favor of laws which reduce workers' access to benefits."[182] Biasing public perception against workers' comp claimants actually serves a dual purpose for insurers: it builds support for reducing benefits, and it discourages workers from filing claims by stigmatizing those who do. Of course, making a false or misleading statement in order to profit at another's expense is the very definition of fraud—and ironically, that definition perfectly fits the practice among insurers of boosting their profits by falsely suggesting that *claimants* commonly commit fraud.

A similar ploy is sometimes used by politicians who oppose government payouts in general, including workers' compensation. A hearing was convened in Washington, D.C. in July 2013 to examine benefit cuts being proposed as part of the Federal Workers' Compensation Modernization and Improvement Act.[183] Subcommittee Chairman Tim Walberg (R-MI) kicked off the meeting by welcoming attendees and reminding them of the hearing's background and purpose. With that out of the way, he said, "As with any government program, there will be those who try to take advantage of the system," and he illustrated his point by calling attention to an article that had been published the previous month in the *Washington Examiner*, titled "Experts say fraud rampant in federal worker disability program."[184] That article had been followed a day later by one titled, "Disability can be easy street for federal bureaucrats," and both were summed up by an editorial that was published the day before the scheduled hearing and began this way:

> Getting federal civil service disability payments can do miraculous things for your health. People too sick to work a desk job have suddenly found themselves able to ski, scuba dive and even run marathons once they started receiving payments from the Federal Employees Compensation Act. That's what Washington

Examiner watchdog reporter Mark Flatten found in a recent three-part investigative series on FECA. The program is rife with fraud.

On Wednesday, the House Education and the Workforce Committee will convene a hearing on efforts to reform FECA. Fraud in FECA has flown under the radar in Congress for far too long. The FECA program costs taxpayers more than $3 billion annually. The Postal Service alone paid out $1.3 billion in FECA compensation last year. The exact amount of fraud isn't clear but the Labor Department's Inspector General has said its "investigations continue to identify high amounts of FECA compensation and medical fraud, which appears to surpass the department's improper payments estimates."[185]

Here the Washington Examiner tore a page from the insurance carriers' playbook by juxtaposing outrageous anecdotes of claimant fraud with high impact dollar amounts that aren't directly relevant, creating the impression of a vast and pressing problem. Once an audience has been baited with the sweet taste of righteous indignation, it can be reeled in with an easy and satisfying solution – some paraphrased rendition of "Let's cut benefits to those lying, cheating scumbags!" But even if workers' compensation fraud were epidemic—which it is not—the obvious solution would be better safeguards against fraud, not punitive benefit cuts that harm honest, rule-following workers the most.

The Inspector General's assertion, as quoted by the *Washington Examiner*, that the FECA underestimates its fraud problem, is from the Office of Inspector General's Semiannual Report spanning October 1, 2012-March 13, 2013. [186] Put in context, the Inspector General's Office was expressing ongoing concerns about improper payments (including both fraud and accidental overpayments) in the Unemployment Insurance, Workforce Investment Act, and FECA programs. Recent fraud cases were described, the biggest by far involving an $11 million kickback scheme by a specialty pharmaceutical company, which victimized not just OWCP but Medicare and other federal health insurance programs as well. OWCP had also been defrauded out of $1.1 million by two men posing as medical providers, and $1.2 million by two actual doctors who over-billed and billed for services not rendered. The claimant fraud cases included a man who was found to be bowling regularly with his supposedly crippled right arm, a woman who failed to report income from a business she operated while accepting disability benefits, and five claimants who submitted falsified travel reimbursement claims. The claimant fraud costs added up to $317,000—far less than the $2.3 million in provider fraud costs, without even accounting for OWCP's share of losses from the $11 million pharmacy kickback scheme. Yet claimant fraud looms much larger in the public imagination, thanks in part to distortions peddled to advance political agendas.

Stigma can be mixed with fear to concoct an even more powerful deterrent to filing claims. In 1999, the Coalition Against Insurance Fraud (CAIF) published a report summarizing its findings and conclusions from an examination of educational outreach materials such as posters and brochures obtained from state fraud bureaus and workers compensation insurance providers.[187] The study found that "much of the material tends to be quite threatening to employees. Strong graphics featuring intimidating colors such as red and black, accompanied by an emphasis on images such as handcuffs, jail cells, stern judges and the like, are the major themes used in these materials." The CAIF also observed that: "None of the materials designed to reach insurers and their employees addressed the issue of premium fraud. This omission would appear to lend some credence to organized labor's frequent complaint that the average worker is the only target and that corporate premium fraud is ignored." Fear tactics in workers' compensation outreach materials send a clear message to workers that it's dangerous to file a claim because authorities will scrutinize every detail, eager for any excuse to prosecute.

The exaggerated emphasis on claimant fraud contributes to a general impression that workers' compensation is a gravy train—an irresistible lure for the injured and non-injured alike. In reality, not only are fraudulent claims extremely rare, but fewer than half of all injured workers who are eligible for benefits claim them.[188] Even workers with serious injuries often choose not to file, as evidenced by studies that collected and compared data from multiple sources on work-related injuries involving amputations. Approximately one-third of California workers whose amputation injuries were recorded in their employers' OSHA logs in 2007 or 2008 didn't file for workers' compensation.[189] In the same timeframe, workers' compensation was listed as primary payer for the hospital bills of only 78% of patients treated for work-related injuries involving amputation in Massachusetts.[190] A myriad of factors can discourage workers from claiming benefits, including lack of awareness or understanding of the process, a belief that filing would be time-consuming, difficult, adversarial, or demeaning; fear of being viewed as a troublemaker or disloyal; fear of being stalked by investigators; fear of employer retaliation or prejudice that will hamper career advancement or lead directly to job loss; embarrassment; desire to maintain medical privacy; peer pressure to help meet "zero injury" goals tied to group incentives; and habit or preference favoring use of private insurance.[191]

The rate of reported nonfatal occupational injuries and illnesses increased gradually from 1982 to 1992, starting at 7.7 occurrences per 100 full-time workers in 1982 and ending at 8.9 in 1992. Then, suddenly, the rate curve executed an abrupt about-face and fell to only 2.8 incidents per 100 full-time workers in 2017 before leveling out.[192] Thus, over the 25-year span from 1992 to 2017, the rate of reported occupational injuries and illnesses plummeted by an incredible 68.5%. Taken at face value, this is great news. But injury reporting is notoriously unreliable; it can be encouraged or discouraged, made easy or difficult, and required by law to greater or lesser extents. Of course, the most extreme outcome of injury is death, and fatalities don't lend themselves well to being either faked or hidden. The rate of reported fatalities didn't exhibit any drastic changes in or around 1992, and in the same 25 years over which the nonfatal occupational injury and illness rate supposedly fell by 68.5%, the fatality rate fell by an impressive but less mind-bending 30%, from five fatalities per 100,000 workers in 1992 to 3.5 in 2017.[193] This strongly suggests that suppressed reporting has contributed at least as much as improved safety to trends observed in data collected over the past quarter century.

Numerous explanations have been offered for the sudden climate change in 1992 that put a chill on workplace injury reporting. One researcher demonstrated a strong correlation with changes in OSHA reporting requirements which made them more lenient.[194] Others pointed to growth of economic insecurity, fueled by high levels of unemployment, crumbling unions, outsourcing of low-skill jobs to low-wage countries, automation, and increasing reliance on a temporary, contingent workforce and an unprotected labor underclass of immigrants. Meanwhile, falling real wages and welfare reform made the consequences of job loss more dire. It stands to reason that people who dread losing their jobs will be less likely to cause trouble by reporting injuries. Peer pressure is being harnessed by employers as well, through the growing use of incentive programs that reward a group of employees for low levels of reported injuries.[195]

Of course, workers' compensation "reform" has also been implicated in the suppression of injury reporting. The various mechanisms by which it accomplishes this include stricter limits on covered conditions, contentious administrative practices combined with restrictive attorney fee limits, shrinking medical provider networks, medical care policies that shift goals away from optimal treatment toward early return to work, demands for full access to claimants' medical information, and stigmatization. One researcher noted bluntly that "a national media campaign in the early 1990s portrayed injured workers as lazy cheats."[196]

The spurious crusade against claimant fraud and the continuous onslaught of cost reduction measures have added their weight to legitimate safety improvements over the past quarter century to make workers' compensation increasingly affordable for employers. In 1993, workers' comp costs accounted for 2.17% of payroll on average, its highest relative cost ever. By 2018, its share had shrunk to only 1.21%. Workers' compensation hasn't been this cheap since the early 1970s, in the era of the National Commission.[197]

"The presumption of widespread malingering and dishonestly undercuts any meaningful discussion of the adequacy of benefits and provides a convenient response for those opposed to the benefit increases that are so critically needed in many states. Until the misplaced focus on claimant fraud is overcome, district attorneys will continue to fry the small fish while the big fish go free, and the voting public will remain distracted by anecdotes. The emphasis on fraud and costs also distracts the public and lawmakers from the workplace hazards and flagrant safety violations that are the real cause of the problem of worker injuries and workers' compensation costs."[198]

- Greg Tarpinian, Executive Director of Labor Research Associates

CHAPTER 18

Double standard

Penalties for federal workers' compensation fraud are defined in Title 18, Sections 1920 through 1922 of the U.S. Code. The original 1966 version of those laws penalized claimant fraud with a fine of up to $2,000, imprisonment for not more than one year, or both. Employers got off a bit easier, with a maximum fine of $500 and up to one year in prison for interfering with the filing of a claim. Incidentally, the penalty prescribed by Section 1919 for fraudulently collecting *unemployment insurance* placed in the middle, earning a maximum fine of $1,000 and up to a year in prison. [199] The penalty for unemployment insurance fraud hasn't changed since 1966, but in September 1994, the penalties for federal workers' compensation fraud were edited by replacing the maximum fine—$500 for employers and $2,000 for claimants—with the phrase "shall be fined under this title," allowing vast leeway within the general Title 18 limits of $250,000 for a felony or a misdemeanor resulting in death, and $100,000 for a misdemeanor not resulting in death. [200]

Just weeks later, still in September 1994, Congress increased the maximum prison term for FECA fraud from one year to five—but not for employers, only for claimants who fraudulently collect benefits in excess of $1,000. [201] The significance of that amendment goes beyond the longer prison term itself. Title 18, Section 3559 of the U.S. Code classifies offenses that are punishable by imprisonment for one year or less as Class A misdemeanors unless otherwise specified. Offenses punishable by imprisonment for five or more years but fewer than ten years are classified by default as Class D felonies.

This means that a federal employer who intentionally cheats an injured employee out of FECA benefits is committing a misdemeanor, and so is any person who lies about federal service to obtain unemployment insurance benefits in any amount. In contrast, an employee who fraudulently obtains more than $1,000 in FECA benefits is committing a felony.

Ohio Revised Code Section 2913.48 prohibits seven specific types of state workers' compensation fraud that encompass acts committed by employees, employers, and providers of goods and services. Prescribed penalties are based not on who committed the crime, but on the monetary amount of unpaid premiums (by employers) or fraudulently obtained benefits (by employees) or payments (by providers). Defrauding Ohio BWC is a first degree misdemeanor for amounts less than $1,000, a fifth degree felony for amounts of at least $1,000 but less than $7,500, a fourth degree felony for amounts of at least $7,500 but less than $150,000, and a third degree felony for amounts of $150,000 or more. Fifth, fourth, and third degree felony convictions carry maximum prison terms of twelve months, eighteen months, and thirty-six months, respectively.

Ohio's penalties for workers' compensation fraud are unbiased, but enforcement is something else altogether. The table below is copied from BWC's Special Investigations Department (SID) Fiscal Year 2019 Annual Report, boasting 101 fraud convictions credited with a total of $65.1 million in savings. The SID was stood up in 1994 (a good year for fraud-fighters) "to proactively detect, investigate, and deter workers' compensation fraud and protect the State Insurance Fund."[202] There are separate SID teams for investigating employer, health-care provider, and claimant fraud.

SID Teams	Prosecution referrals	Indictments	Convictions	Identified savings
Employer	69	63	53	$15,415,430
Health-care	7	6	4	$5,065,993
Claimant	113	50	44	$44,662,898
Total	189	119	101	$65,144,322

Table: Ohio BWC Special Investigation Department
Activity in Fiscal Year 2019[203]

The "Identified savings" column takes credit not just for actual amounts defrauded, but also future losses that might have been avoided by the convictions. BWC accepted 84,364 claims in Fiscal Year 2019,[204] so the 44 claimant convictions represent a miniscule fraud rate of 0.05%. Nevertheless, claimant fraud receives a lot of attention. The introductory page of BWC's Fiscal Year 2019 report begins this way:

> This report documents actions we took in fiscal year 2019 (FY19) to improve the quality of life for Ohio's workers and to be a positive influence for economic growth in Ohio. Our focus on preventing workplace accidents, lowering rates, and caring for those injured on the job is making Ohio a better place for businesses and workers. This focus and our commitment to the principles of service, simplicity, and savings helped us operate efficiently during FY19.[205]

As a subliminal reminder of BWC's true focus, two graphics are planted above this text: handcuffs and a handcuff key. A graphic below depicts a person holding up a giant dollar bill. In addition to seeing to it that Ohio citizens who are injured on their jobs receive the compensation they are due in accordance with the Grand Bargain, BWC self-proclaims responsibility for being "a positive influence for economic growth in Ohio," "lowering rates," and "making Ohio a better place for businesses." Who wins when the best interests of injured workers are at odds with those of their employers?

Most of BWC's Fiscal Year 2019 fraud convictions are described briefly in the SID's blog. Only three of those cases conform to the popular stereotype of workers' compensation fraud. One woman had been collecting her late father's BWC benefits for two years. She was convicted of a felony and of course had to pay back the ill-gotten $29,418.[206] One man was a former county deputy sheriff who intentionally deceived BWC and his physician to claim benefits. He owed back $211,536 and was also ordered to compensate BWC $23,187 for investigation costs.[207] Another woman submitted a false statement to support her claim for workers' comp benefits. She had collected nothing before getting caught, so only had to pay a $250 fine and reimburse BWC $128 for their investigation.[208]

All the other convicted claimants whose stories are told in the BWC SID's blog were found guilty only of working for extra money while collecting disability benefits, and failing to report it. None were accused of faking or exaggerating their injuries. Presumably they really *had* been injured at work and had some degree of disability due to those injuries. They broke the law, but not in the way we've all been trained to assume. While accepting compensation from BWC for their lost earning potential, they made extra money through honest work, typically part-time or intermittently. Many drove trucks or were self-employed as a travel agent, photographer, electrician, or general contractor. Others were hired by restaurants, offices, and manufacturers.

The SID's table of Fiscal Year 2019 anti-fraud activity makes claimant fraud appear to be a bigger problem than employer fraud. Although there were more convictions of employers than claimants, the total associated cost saving shown is greater for the claimant convictions. But there's data missing from the table. To understand what it is, you first need to know what procedures are followed when BWC identifies an employer who is not paying his workers' compensation premiums. Unlike claimant and provider fraud, which are prosecuted without delay, a series of steps take place when addressing non-compliance of an employer. The process is defined in Ohio Administrative Code Section 4123-14-02 and is summarized below:

1. BWC provides written notice to the employer that he has 20 days to furnish the Bureau with a payroll report and pay into the state insurance fund the amount of premium and assessments applicable to the time period for which he has been non-compliant.

2. If Step One fails, BWC makes an assessment of the amount due based on information in its possession, provides that assessment to the employer, and gives him 20 days to either pay the assessed amount or file a written petition objecting to it.

3. If Step Two fails, BWC mails a copy of its final assessment to the employer and files a lien in the common pleas court of any county in which the employer has property or a place of business. The employer must make payment within ten days or risk having his property seized, though he has a right to appeal the administrator's decision to the court of common pleas of Franklin county.

BWC doesn't disclose how many employers it threatens with foreclosure after they ignore two separate notices of payment due. Luckily, that information is published on many county court websites. In Fiscal Year 2019, BWC filed more than 4,000 liens against businesses in Ohio's four most populous counties alone: Franklin, Cuyahoga, Hamilton, and Summit, which together contain about a third of Ohio's population. Clearly, BWC's biggest fraud problem by far is employers not paying their premiums. Nevertheless, BWC pursued charges against only 53 of those 4,000+ non-compliant business owners. The SID blog makes it clear that BWC prosecutes employers with great reluctance, as a very last resort. Business owner James Wilson was convicted of fraud in November 2018 for neglecting to pay his premiums. He had been convicted of the same thing nine years earlier, at which time he had owed $180,000. The SID blog writer doesn't share how far in arrears Mr. Wilson slipped this time, but conveys BWC's grief over what transpired next:

> "We attempted to work with Mr. Wilson to bring his business into compliance with Ohio law, but ultimately we had to go with this course of action," said Jim Wernecke, director of BWC's special investigations department. "I can't say this enough to employers in our system: If you're struggling with your BWC premiums,

reach out to our agency and work with us. Don't risk a criminal conviction."[209]

Mr. Wernecke's heartfelt plea to struggling employers is repeated later in the same blog post, following more sad stories like poor Mr. Wilson's:

> "We made every attempt to bring these employers into compliance with Ohio law, but they wouldn't cooperate and we were forced to bring charges against them," said Jim Wernecke, director of BWC's special investigations department (SID). "I can't stress this to employers enough: If you're struggling with your BWC premiums, work with us. Avoiding us will only make your situation worse."[210]

BWC's tone differs strikingly when commenting on *claimant* fraud. In January 2019, Ohio resident Dawn Hattery was caught working as a receptionist while simultaneously collecting a total of $17,937 in BWC benefits over the course of 11 months. She pleaded guilty and was required to pay back the entire amount of compensation she had received while working, plus another $1,000 to cover BWC's investigative costs. BWC did not dispute the fact that she had been injured and rightfully entitled to compensation, but she broke the law by earning extra income and not reporting it. Now she has debt, a disability, and a felony record to boot. BWC Administrator/CEO Stephanie McCloud gloated: "Ms. Hattery not only broke the law deceiving this agency, she earned a criminal record that will follow her for years to come. Our role is to compensate workers while they're recovering from injury, not pad the income of people trying to cheat the system."[211]

Slight variations on the canned scolding above are repeated regularly in the SID's blog and annual reports, aimed at an ever-changing lineup of villainous "income-padding" claimants who commit a crime BWC calls "working while receiving." In the very same month Ms. Hattery was pilloried for supposedly hoarding scarce resources away from injured workers who needed and deserved them more, BWC announced a proposal to reduce the average premium rate it charges private employers by 20% — its largest rate cut in nearly 60 years. According to the press release:

> If approved by the board at its meeting Feb. 22, the rate reduction would be effective July 1 and save private employers $244 million over premiums for fiscal year 2019. The proposed cut would follow a 12 percent reduction last year and a pattern of no increases since 2006. It would also follow a 12 percent rate reduction for public employers – counties, cities, schools and others – that went into effect Jan. 1. Overall, the average rate levels for the 242,000 Ohio employers in the BWC system are at their lowest in at least 40 years.[212]

BWC's Board of Directors approved the premium cut in February 2019. A few months later, Governor Mike DeWine and BWC Administrator/CEO Stephanie McCloud jointly announced a proposed $1.5 billion rebate for Ohio employers — equal to 88% of total premiums paid the previous year, and the fifth rebate of $1 billion or more issued by BWC to Ohio's employers since 2013. Governor DeWine had this to say about it: "We are committed to providing resources for Ohio businesses to expand, support their employees, and become stronger competitors in the global marketplace. Because of BWC's leadership and strong investments, Ohio employers will now have the opportunity to make additional investments in their businesses." Ms. McCloud parroted her boss: "We are grateful and more than pleased to once again be in a strong fiscal position that allows us to send these dollars to Ohio employers. Our hope is employers will reinvest these dollars into their companies, particularly in the area of workplace safety, and help our economy continue to prosper."[213]

Like all state governors, Ohio's governor is beholden to the business owners who played a role in helping him get elected and might help him be re-elected. Naturally, a major component of a governor's score card is the economic health of his state, which depends on attracting and keeping businesses. It's understandable that a state governor would tend to display much greater leniency toward business owners than toward laborers. It's also unsurprising that Ohio's governor and its workers' compensation administrator speak as one – Ohio law provides that the governor shall appoint the BWC Administrator and can fire him or her at will.[214]

Samuel Horovitz was a 1922 Harvard Law School graduate who quickly found his calling in the plight of the many unrepresented workers who waged battle alone against skilled lawyers and doctors representing their employers. Mr. Horovitz devoted his career to advocating for injured workers.[215] In 1944, he wrote a book to educate lawyers and laymen alike, titled *Injury and Death under Workmen's Compensation Laws*. Horovitz favored exclusive state funds over allowing employers to purchase private insurance, writing that "an exclusive state fund in place of carriers is not a hundred per cent solution, but it will go a great way in aiding workers. The profit motive is removed."[216] Perhaps he gave state fund administrators too much credit. They have a political motive that can be every bit as pernicious as a profit motive. Horovitz may have been somewhat blinded by his own idealism; he wrote that "administrators must resist all inroads on their integrity" and echoed Harvard Law Professor Zechariah Chafee, Jr.'s view that true independence implies an ability to "look the whole world in the face from the governor down to the mob, and tell them all to 'go to h---.'"[217]

"Workers' compensation is an unfortunate example of how a seemingly fair program can be manipulated by political forces into a nightmare for those it was originally meant to help. Once an area of law is removed from the civil justice system, it becomes vulnerable to money, politics and influence-peddling. This happens either through aggressive industry lobbying of legislators, political influence on the agencies charged with implementing the system, or orchestrated media efforts. All have happened to workers' compensation."[218]

-Amy Widman, Center for Justice and Democracy

CHAPTER 19

Don't do anything productive for the rest of your life

Social Security Disability Insurance (SSDI) was rolled out in 1956 to provide income for Americans below retirement age who become unable to support themselves because of a disability that is expected to result in death or last for at least one year. The disability doesn't have to be work-related, but an applicant must have worked a certain number of years in a recent timeframe; exact work history requirements depend on the applicant's age, and benefit amount depends on his or her pre-disability salary. Unlike workers' compensation, which has a waiting period of seven days at most, SSDI has a waiting period of five months post-injury; after another 24 months, Medicare kicks in. Curious to know how SSDI compares with workers' compensation, I attended a class hosted by my employing agency. Shortly into her presentation, the instructor made a comment that helped me better understand just what it is I find so repugnant about the strict and punitive way BWC and OWCP enforce disability in their beneficiaries. She said: "As normal humans, we're wired to want to do something." Isn't that (thankfully) true? I don't believe many people could happily go through life accomplishing and contributing nothing.

Workers' compensation beneficiaries receive wage replacement payments if they are either temporarily or permanently unable to perform a job that pays as well as the one on which they were injured; one catch is that they must limit all their activities and endeavors or risk losing the entire benefit amount once and for all. In 1926, U.S. Employees Compensation Commissioner Charles Verrill told Congress:

> There is the conscious and deliberate malingerer, and more numerous, I believe, is the unconscious malingerer, who is influenced oftentimes by the fear that if he goes back to work his compensation will be cut off finally, and that if he honestly goes to work and tries to work and fails, why, he cannot get any compensation afterward.
>
> Of course, that is an utterly erroneous idea; but frankly, I am sure it influences a good many men. The effect of the man's attitude toward the continuance of compensation is very serious upon his morale. It is a question of psychology that one finds it difficult to understand, until he has seen numerous cases. One would not think that any person would voluntarily refrain from work and accept $66.67 a month if he could go to work and get much more money. And yet we know it does happen. We do know that men submit to surgical operations for the sake of getting continuance of the compensation.
>
> Of course, I think I may say that those are the "freaks"; but the world has got a good many freaks in it.[219]

A partial solution proposed by Mr. Verrill was to implement schedule awards (described in Chapter 9), in order "to make it certain what a man will get if he has an amputation, or something in the way of partial disability quite as definite as that ... the certainty, as opposed to the uncertainty, permits the disabled man to immediately think of getting back into industry and doing all he can to become self-supporting, just as the other in a way encourages or naturally results in the thought that getting back to work too soon may prejudice the amount of money to be received."[220]

Most states allow negotiation of compromise and release settlements, whereby the injured employee receives an agreed-upon lump sum or series of payments, then his or her case is closed, with no more benefits available. In addition to saving administrative costs, settlements have the same advantage as schedule awards in that they free the beneficiary from having to prove continued disability in order to receive compensation, making it easier for him or her to move forward. Potentially, a lump sum can be invested in vocational training of the employee's choice or start-up costs for a small business. There are also strong arguments against settlement of workers' compensation claims, such as the fact that lump sum settlements tend to favor the insurer and may not cover all of the beneficiary's future medical bills and lost wages, and that they might be squandered.

Though the amount of wage replacement awarded has always depended on lost earning ability, and overpayments or improper payments when discovered were always demanded repaid, FECA beneficiaries haven't always been criminally prosecuted for earning supplemental income. When Commissioner Verrill was asked in 1923 by House Representative Hatton Sumners (D-TX) how that situation was handled, he replied matter-of-factly, with none of the demonizing fraud rhetoric commonly used today:

> Mr. Sumners: How do you check up on this proposition where a man engaged in one of the Government activities contracts a vocational disease and is put on your pay roll and quits work, but engages in some independent activity—possibly opens up a little grocery store on the corner near his place, as an illustration.

> Mr. Verrill: Yes; if that should happen, and it does happen sometimes, we would require an affidavit to show what he was earning and make an investigation if necessary and we would hold, in accordance with the law, that he was entitled to not more than two-thirds of his loss of earnings which was the result of his disability. If

it was not shown that it was a result of the disability we would pay him nothing.[221]

Some state system beneficiaries were even explicitly allowed to make extra money without sacrificing benefits. In 1922, the New York Supreme Court heard the case of McCann v. McCormack's Garage.[222] Mr. McCann had previously worked as a chauffeur and mover until he was hit by a car while in the road cranking his truck. He recovered partially, but not enough to return to his original job, and so he was awarded compensation. He started a trucking business, with other men working for him and an office staffed by his wife. The profit he made from the business, $35 per week, equaled the wage he had been earning at the time of his injury. The workers' compensation insurance carrier argued that it should no longer have to pay him, since he was no longer experiencing reduced income. However, the court ruled in favor of Mr. McCann on the grounds that income from a business venture or investments should not be counted against a claimant, as it had nothing to do with his "wage-earning capacity," defined as the rate he could reasonably expect to be paid by another in exchange for his labor:

> Income or profits from business are not the fruits of wage-earning capacity. It is sometimes said that a man who owns and manages a large business earns what he receives as a return from that business, but not at all in the sense that those returns are the result of his wage-earning capacity. The profits are the return from the investment, the management, the business capacity of this owner; and some years he may receive a profit of forty per cent and other years he suffers a loss. The profit from his business is in no sense a measure of his wage-earning capacity.[223]

OWCP and BWC both require claimants who receive wage replacement benefits to periodically report not only their earnings, but also their volunteer activities, based on the reasoning that even unpaid work can indicate earning potential. Sometimes the quest to ferret out ability crosses over into a claimant's personal life. Kristi Ness was a mail carrier who underwent partial knee replacement required due to a work injury. Ms. Ness was ordered by her doctor to remain off work for 8 to 12 weeks afterward. During that recovery period, fraud investigators secretly videotaped her as she helped her husband repair his mother's sprinkler, digging with a shovel. Video also showed her assisting with a construction project he was doing for a family friend; she dug and carried lumber, taking breaks to stretch her leg and do physical therapy exercises. Ms. Ness was charged with workers' compensation fraud, tried, and ultimately acquitted — after her doctor testified that he had told her to let her body be her guide post-surgery and he saw nothing unseemly about her activity level; and after her mother-in-law testified that she had not paid for the sprinkler repair, nor would she have paid someone else to do it if her son and daughter-in-law had not been willing; and after her husband testified that he did not pay her for helping him on the job site or for performing chores at home, such as washing dishes.[224]

Workers' compensation administrators have a powerful incentive to prosecute claimant fraud and to define it broadly. A claimant who is convicted of "fraud" for earning an unreported dollar on the side over a period of time during which he or she accepted $1,000 in disability payments must pay back not just $1 but $1,000, and also forfeits all future benefits related to the same injury; FECA claimants who are convicted of fraud stop receiving benefits for any other past injury as well.[225] That's a bonanza for the administrator. A LexisNexis analysis found that "workers' compensation is harsher on fraud than in civil cases. Civil cases use a balancing test, i.e., how bad is the misrepresentation versus the claim, whereas in workers' compensation, it is an absolute."[226] Scorched earth consequences might seem justified in the context of stereotypical claimant fraud, where the claimant has no real basis for entitlement to benefits. More common, though, is the partially disabled claimant who supplements meager benefits by working on the side, without necessarily exceeding his or her documented medical restrictions.

The "absolute" bar for claimant fraud makes no rational distinction between the stereotypical and truly typical scenarios.

Social Security administrators are apparently less motivated to withhold and take back benefits. Although Social Security Disability Insurance generally pays less than workers' compensation, it allows beneficiaries to supplement with other income as long as those earnings fall short of a limit that counts as Substantial Gainful Activity (SGA); the SGA limit in 2020 was $1260 per month, or $2110 for the blind. What's more, SSDI addresses the legitimate fears of beneficiaries in a constructive rather than punitive manner by offering a nine-month trial work period during which they can test their money-making ability, and keep all the money they earn, without risk of losing their benefits. If a beneficiary's earnings during the trial period exceed the SGA limit, benefits are paid on a month-by-month basis as needed, depending on each month's earnings, for three years before being suspended altogether. Even then, there is a fast-track process for reinstating them if necessary, giving beneficiaries peace of mind that they won't ultimately sink themselves by trying to do without help.

Another alternative to workers' compensation for some disabled federal civilian employees is Federal Disability Retirement (FDR), available to workers with at least 18 months of service who become unable to perform their current job or any available same-grade job in their employing agency because of a medical condition that is expected to last at least one year. The disability does not have to be job-related, though it can be. FDR pays 60% of the employee's highest three-year average salary the first year, and 40% every year thereafter until age 62, at which time regular retirement benefits commence, calculated with service credit for time under the FDR program. There is no pressure to play dead: an FDR beneficiary is allowed to earn up to 80% of his pre-disability retirement salary as long as his medical restrictions are not exceeded. If he is found to be earning more than that, he is not charged with fraud and forced to pay it all back; in fact, he continues receiving FDR benefits until six months from the end of the calendar year in which his earning capacity was restored, or until the date he is reemployed in the federal service, whichever comes first.[227]

I see no reason to think human nature is any better or any worse now than it was before the enactment of workers' compensation laws, when employers dodged the consequences of workplace accidents by taking cover behind the unholy trinity of common law defenses. The last vestige of those defenses, reluctantly abandoned by some employers, was the practice of making new hires sign away their right to sue if injured on the job (known as "workers' right to die contracts").[228] When workers' compensation laws went into full effect, employers sought new ways to reduce costs and boost profits; that's just what employers do. Proven strategies now include using threats or incentives to discourage the filing of claims, limiting access to medical care and legal representation, and crying fraud at every opportunity. Both the extent and the nature of workers' compensation fraud are intentionally misrepresented to the public in order to garner support for policies and laws that are cruel to injured workers but profitable for employers—much like the old common law defenses were.

"The intent of the founders of compensation acts to give wide relief to injured workers receives many a jolt as new decisions seek new ways of denying recovery."[229]

-Samuel Horovitz, Attorney and worker advocate, 1944

CHAPTER 20

Good intentions

As described in previous chapters, a limited-scope federal employees' compensation law was enacted in 1908 that covered only employees in especially hazardous jobs; covered occupational injuries only, not diseases; provided wage replacement only for a limited duration; and did not pay for medical treatment. The 1908 law was supplanted in 1916 by a more comprehensive law[230] that covered virtually all federal civilian employees who sustained any work-related disability or death, providing them with replacement wages and medical treatment for as long as needed. The Secretary of Labor had administered the original act, but the new one was administered by the gold-standard entity for independent, unbiased adjudication: a commission made up of three members with diverse political views, who served staggered terms and whose appointments required Senate approval so as not to be controlled by any one government official or political party. Section 28 of the 1916 act specified:

> **SEC. 28.** That a commission is hereby created, to be known as the United States Employees' Compensation Commission, and to be composed of three commissioners appointed by the President, by and with the advice and consent of the Senate, one of whom shall be designated by the President as chairman. No commissioner shall hold any other office or position under the United States. No more than two of said commissioners shall be members of the same political party. One of said

commissioners shall be appointed for a term of two years, one for a term of four years, and one for a term of six years, and at the expiration of each of said terms, the commissioner then appointed shall be appointed for a period of six years.

The newly formed U.S. Employees' Compensation Commission had full authority over defining policy and adjudicating claims:

SEC. 32. That the commission is authorized to make necessary rules and regulations for the enforcement of this Act, and shall decide all questions arising under this Act.

SEC. 37. That if the original claim for compensation has been made within the time specified in section twenty, the commission may, at any time, on its own motion or on application, review the award, and, in accordance with the facts found on such review, may end, diminish, or increase the compensation previously awarded, or, if compensation has been refused or discontinued, award compensation.

The intention of Section 37 was to make the commissioners comfortable erring on the side of swiftly providing necessary relief to claimants, with the understanding that they would always be free to later reverse their decisions and secure repayment of mistaken awards."[231]

The already expansive authority given to the Commission was made even more so in 1924 by appending the following verbiage to Section 37:

In the absence of fraud or mistake in mathematical calculations, the finding of facts in, and the decision of the commission upon, the merits of any claim presented under or authorized by this Act if supported by competent evidence shall not be subject to review by any other administrative or accounting officer, employee, or agent of the United States.[232]

The above amendment was prompted by the commissioners' frustration with Comptroller General J.R. McCarl, who was refusing to pay out any benefits for occupational diseases, based on his own interpretation of the law.[233] The wording of the Act as adopted in 1916 was undeniably ambiguous in this regard, stating "that the United States shall pay compensation as hereinafter specified for the disability or death of an employee resulting from a personal injury sustained while in the performance of his duty." However, it had been made clear in the hearings leading up to enactment that the term "personal injury" was meant to include occupational diseases, and broad wording was intentionally chosen to allow the commissioners as much latitude as possible. Dr. Royal Meeker, former administrator of the 1908 act, had felt especially strongly about covering diseases under the 1916 act, testifying: "What is the difference between being laid up for six weeks because of a broken leg and being laid up for six weeks because of pleurisy contracted during employment? For myself I can see no difference. The grocery bills are coming in just the same in the one case as in the other. The rent has to be paid, and the expense of supporting the injured workman's family goes on in one case just the same as in the other. I see no reason for excluding occupational diseases."[234]

The cases for which Mr. McCarl refused to release funds included survivor benefits for the family of a 28-year-old rural letter carrier who froze to death on his route after a sudden change in weather, and for the family of a 15-year-old boy who died of T.N.T. poisoning after working for two months in a munitions plant where his repeated requests for a protective dust mask were ignored by the foreman. The Section 37 amendment, drafted for the express purpose of throttling Mr. McCarl's influence over benefit awards, didn't originally contain the phrase "or accounting officer." It specified only that the Commission's determinations could not be overruled by "any other administrative officer, employee, or agent of the United States." In a long letter defending his viewpoint, Mr. McCarl scoffed at that choice of wording, writing:

> The office of Comptroller General of the United States, created by the budget and accounting act of June 10, 1921, with authority to direct the audit of expenditures of appropriated funds and settlement of claims against the United States, could not be considered as coming within the term "other administrative officer, employee, or agent of the United States."

The amendment's sponsor, Hon. William Vaile (R-CO), countered by inserting the words "or accounting officer." The bill was approved. In addition to amending Section 37 as just described, it explicitly defined the term "injury" to include, "in addition to injury by accident, any disease proximately caused by the employment."[235]

Comptroller General McCarl soon found a new way to foil the commissioners, this time by refusing to release funds for prosthetic devices because there was no mention of them in Section 9 of the Act, which began:

> **SEC. 9.** That immediately after an injury sustained by an employee while in the performance of his duty, whether or not disability has arisen, and for a reasonable time thereafter, the United States shall furnish to such employee reasonable medical, surgical, and hospital services and supplies unless he refuses to accept them.

In 1926, at the request of the commissioners, Congress revised the Section 9 wording to explicitly cover appliances and furthermore to give the Employees' Compensation Commission ultimate authority over which medical treatments were compensable. Gone was the word "reasonable," and in its place was "in the opinion of the Commission." I emphasize that new wording with bold font below:

SEC. 9. That for any injury sustained by an employee while in the performance of duty, whether or not disability has arisen, the United States shall furnish to the employee all services, **appliances**, and supplies prescribed or recommended by duly qualified physicians which, **in the opinion of the Commission**, are likely to cure or to give relief or to reduce the degree or the period of disability or to aid in lessening the amount of the monthly compensation."[236]

Commission Chairperson Bessie Brueggeman got a laugh from the Congressmen by ending her testimony in support of that amendment with a jab at Mr. McCarl: "And in conclusion, I wish to say last, but not least, the commissioners will again have to bring to your attention the fact that we have a Comptroller General of the United States, who resembles in one respect, at least, the poor of this land, in that we always have him with us."[237] He must have stayed in his own lane after that, though, because he inspired no more amendments.

The first sentence of today's FECA law in 5 U.S.C. 8103 substantially mirrors the Section 9 wording settled upon in 1926, except that approval of medical treatment no longer rides on the opinion of a commission, but rather that of the Secretary of Labor:

5 U.S.C. 8103. Medical services and initial medical and other benefits

(a) The United States shall furnish to an employee who is injured while in the performance of duty, the services, appliances, and supplies prescribed or recommended by a qualified physician, which **the Secretary of Labor considers** likely to cure, give relief, reduce the degree or the period of disability, or aid in lessening the amount of the monthly compensation.

Ironically, the unimpeachable power fought for and won by the Employees' Compensation Commission so it could shield beneficiaries from an interfering political appointee, the Comptroller General, was handed over whole in 1950 to a different political appointee, the Secretary of Labor. The next chapter explains how that happened.

CHAPTER 21

Presidential power grabs

President Herbert Hoover was frustrated by the sluggish pace of Congressional approval for new legislation and by Congress' tendency to amend proposed laws beyond recognition. Consequently, when he had the idea to reorganize the executive branch of government in ways he thought would make it more efficient, he didn't go through the usual legislative process but instead asked Congress to delegate the necessary reorganization power to him. Congress obliged in 1932, granting him power to transfer executive agencies in whole or in part between departments, and to consolidate or redistribute their functions. There were stipulations: he could not abolish an entire department or agency that had been created by statute, and any executive order he issued would have a waiting period of 60 days before going into effect, during which time either the Senate or the House of Representatives could vote it down. Also, the President's new power could be exercised only toward the end of accomplishing specific goals declared by Congress: grouping and consolidating federal agencies according to major purpose, reducing the number of agencies, eliminating overlapping and duplication of effort among agencies, and segregating regulatory agencies from administrative or executive agencies.[238]

President Hoover issued 11 executive orders directing the reorganization of various agencies according to major functions. However, by the time he did so, he had already been defeated in his bid for reelection by Franklin D. Roosevelt, and the House of

Representatives disapproved all of Hoover's executive orders, mainly out of reluctance to force sweeping changes on a new President who hadn't chosen them. President Hoover expressed a wish that Congress would grant his successor greater reorganization power than he had enjoyed, and the onset of the Great Depression lent a sense of urgency to economizing government operations. Accordingly, just before Hoover left office in 1933, Congress extended presidential reorganization authority for two more years and surrendered its option to overrule the President's reorganization orders. Additionally, the list of approved goals for any plan was expanded to include reducing expenditures and abolishing unnecessary agencies or functions. President Roosevelt issued numerous executive orders regrouping and abolishing various agencies and functions before the amendment expired in 1935.[239]

In 1939, President Roosevelt negotiated renewed reorganization authority from Congress. By the terms of this agreement, his initiatives would have to be issued in the form of reorganization plans, not executive orders. As with President Hoover's 1932 powers, any such plan could be nullified within 60 days, but this time only by a concurrent resolution in both Congressional chambers—House and Senate—not just one or the other. Twenty-one agencies were declared off limits for inclusion in any reorganization plan, and the U.S. Employees' Compensation Commission was one of them. Roosevelt issued five plans, all of which went into effect.[240]

President Roosevelt's Reorganization Plan No. 1 of 1939 declared two related goals: "This Plan is concerned with the practical necessity of reducing the number of agencies which report directly to the President and also of giving the President assistance in dealing with the entire Executive Branch by modern means of administrative management."[241] The plan is best known for creating the Executive Office of the President to guide and support the President's policies, but it also created the Federal Works Agency, the Federal Loan Agency, and the Federal Security Agency (FSA). The FSA was an independent agency established "to promote social and economic security, educational opportunity, and the health of the citizens of the Nation."[242] It consolidated the already existing Social Security Board, U.S. Employment Service, Public Health Service, Office of Education, Civilian Conservation Corps, and National Youth Administration.

The only one of Roosevelt's five plans to face serious challenge was Reorganization Plan No. 4 of 1940, which was disapproved by the House of Representatives but not the Senate. As Hon. Walter Judd (R-MN) later recounted, "It was under that law which the House had disapproved that the [Civil Aeronautics Authority] was placed under the Department of Commerce, so that it ceased to be a wholly independent quasi-judicial agency and became subject to the control of the Secretary of Commerce, who is a political appointee." To the dismay of Mr. Judd and his like-minded colleagues, the Senate endorsed Reorganization Plan No. 4, and it was enacted.[243]

An understanding of the House's objection to Reorganization Plan No 4 of 1940 requires some understanding of what it means for an agency to be "independent." The executive branch of the U.S. Federal Government encompasses 15 executive departments, including the Department of Commerce and the Department Labor, as well as numerous independent agencies. Each executive department is headed by a Secretary who is part of the President's Cabinet of advisors. Cabinet Secretaries generally serve until the end of the term of the President who appointed them, but they can be dismissed by the President at any time, without cause. Presidents have less control over the heads of independent agencies, whose authority and responsibilities are established through laws approved by Congress. Independent agencies are commonly led by a commission or board consisting of 3 to 7 members who serve staggered terms. Board members might be nominated by the President and confirmed by the Senate just as Cabinet Secretaries are, but they can be dismissed only with just cause, such as incapacity or neglect of duty. They commonly serve terms that span more than one president, giving the agency greater stability in addition to its independence.

World War II kept President Roosevelt too busy to pursue having his reorganization authority renewed when it expired at the end of 1940. That power lay dormant until Harry S. Truman requested it soon after entering office in 1945. After some negotiation, Congress granted it to him. The terms of this agreement were similar to those of the 1939 Act, with similar options at the President's disposal and a concurrent resolution from both House and Senate needed to overrule any of his plans. The list of approved goals for any plan was appended with: "To facilitate orderly transition from war to peace." The list of 21 agencies declared off limits by the 1939 Act was whittled down to just 11 in the 1945 Act, and the Employees' Compensation Commission was not among them; however, the Commission was (at least in theory) afforded some indirect protection by a new clause that guarded the independent discretion of agencies responsible for making rules and regulations (called quasi-legislative functions) or conducting hearings and investigations (called quasi-judicial functions):

> **Section 5. (a)** No reorganization plan shall provide for, and no reorganization under this Act shall have the effect of—...**(6)** imposing, in connection with the exercise of any quasi-judicial or quasi-legislative function possessed by an independent agency, any greater limitation upon the exercise of independent judgment and discretion, to the full extent authorized by law, in the carrying out of such function, than existed with respect to the exercise of such function by the agency in which it was vested prior to the taking effect of such reorganization; except that this prohibition shall not prevent the abolition of any such function."[244]

President Truman submitted seven reorganization plans to Congress over the next several years, three of which were blocked by concurrent resolutions and four of which were enacted. Truman's

Plan No. 2 of 1946 was divided into 12 sections; Section 3 abolished the Employees' Compensation Commission and transferred its functions to the Federal Security Agency created by Roosevelt in 1939. In his message transmitting Plan No. 2 of 1946 to Congress, President Truman explained:

> The plan transfers the functions of the United States Employees Compensation Commission to the Federal Security Administrator, and provides for a three-member board of appeals to hear and finally decide appeals on claims of Government employees. By abolishing the Commission, the plan eliminates a small agency and lightens the burden on the President. The Federal Security Administrator, as the head of the Federal agency with the greatest experience in insurance administration, is in the best position to guide and further the program of the Commission.[245]

The House of Representatives drafted resolutions to reject Reorganization Plan No. 2 of 1946, along with unrelated Plans No. 1 and 3 which it received at the same time. Hearings on the resolutions were held from June 4th through the 13th, 1946.[246] The plans were defended by Harold D. Smith, Director of the Bureau of the Budget which had taken the lead in preparing them; and by George T. Washington, Acting Assistant Solicitor General, whose Justice Department had contributed legal guidance. Dozens of stakeholders testified in opposition to Section 3 of Plan No. 2, which would abolish the Employees' Compensation Commission. In addition to administering the 1916 Federal Employees' Compensation Act, the Commission also administered the 1927 Longshore and Harbor Workers Compensation Act. Leaders of the International Longshoremen's Association praised the "honest, sincere and efficient directors and commissioners" and expressed strong opposition on behalf of their 15,000 members to seeing the Commission disbanded.[247] This sentiment was echoed by several other witnesses and captured most vividly by Clarence Stinson, who represented the National Association of Letter Carriers:

> "We have got a wonderfully efficient agency and you propose to set up something untried and unknown. It appears to me somewhat similar to an epitaph that appears on a tombstone up in the Boston cemetery. It runs something like this: "I was well. I wanted to be better. I saw a doctor and here I am."[248]

Questions were raised as to whether Section 3 served any of the reorganization objectives authorized by Congress, such as reducing expenditures, increasing efficiency, or facilitating orderly transition from war to peace. The plan's purported advantage of lightening the burden on the President was dismissed by Government Employees' Councilman George Riley:

> There will never be an agency of Government which has done a better job than the United States Employees Compensation Commission to lighten that famous "burden on the President." This Commission is never heard from except when time comes to submit its annual report. It never gets in anybody's hair. It does not specialize in hiring any persons of questionable American-line leanings. It tends to its assigned business and keeps too well occupied to mix in with anything in which it is not concerned.
>
> But it is often true, even in the case of an individual, that those who work the hardest and with a minimum of noise reap the reward of failure to politic in the right places with the right persons.
>
> As a matter of fact, I believe this committee will find if it will call for the White House calling lists as far back as 1916 when this Commission was created, that there have been only six times when any members of this Commission ever called to see the President or were invited except at social functions. So, it can hardly be said that this Commission has soaked up any of the official

time of the President whose "burden" the Bureau of the Budget has decided it has to lighten.[249]

Reservations were expressed about lumping workmen's compensation together with welfare programs, which differed markedly in philosophy and execution. In the words of Congressman E.C. Hallbeck, legislative representative of the National Federation of Post Office Clerks: "Under the proposed new method of administration, the compensation law will be merged with the administration of a general welfare program. This is a new concept of workmen's compensation. It is a radical departure from the universally accepted view that workmen's compensation benefits is [sic] a substantial fundamental 'right' and not a gratuitous grant or insurance plan for relief or welfare. It is the substituted right of an employee against his employer for the older common law action."[250]

The greatest point of contention over Section 3 of Plan No. 2 was the loss of independence and the opportunity for bias introduced by trading a politically diverse commission of three non-government-connected persons for a single administrator who could be challenged only by a three-member appeals board of his own choosing. Weakening of independence was a weighty consideration because there was general agreement that the Employees' Compensation Commission acted as a quasi-judicial body in its role of determining eligibility for benefits, and the Reorganization Act of 1945 explicitly forbade imposing any greater limitation on the judgment and discretion of any quasi-judicial agency. Mr. Riley was one of many who objected along those lines:

> In this Reorganization Order No. 2 there is language which gives the Federal Security Administrator authority to perform the present functions of the Commission "in such manner and under such rules and regulations" as he may prescribe. Such blanket authority places no limitation upon his powers and obviously leaves to his discretion any changes in administration as he may decide upon.

The Board of Appeals provided for under this plan is a creation of the Agency Administrator and serves at his pleasure. Consequently, such Board lacks all of the semblance of autonomy essential for the exercise of free and independent judgment. And by its origin, it likewise is susceptible to partisan control and personal politics.[251]

Some who took part in the debate challenged the constitutionality of any reorganization act that grants legislative powers to a president and requires Congress to take active measures within a fixed timeframe to prevent his plans from going into effect. The Constitution grants Congress the exclusive power to legislate, and in accordance with the doctrine of separation of powers, Congress cannot abdicate that power or delegate it to others.[252] In fact, the "legislative veto" that was a key element of expedited reorganization authority granted to nine presidents over the course of 52 years was ruled unconstitutional in 1983 and is no longer viable.[253]

The resolution against Plan No. 2 was approved by the House[254] but still faced debate in the Senate. There was a weaker turnout of the plan's Section 3 opponents before the Senate, with Government Employees' Councilman George Riley doing most of the heavy lifting; still, the Senate heard much of the same testimony the House had heard in praise the Employees' Compensation Commission and questioning the wisdom of changing a process that was unanimously thought to be working quite well. There was continued discussion regarding the unsuitability of lumping workers' compensation with welfare and the lack of any apparent benefit to doing so. The constitutionality of allowing Congress to delegate its legislative power to the President via reorganization acts was challenged again, as was the legality of weakening the independence of the Employees' Compensation Commission by transferring ownership of its quasi-judicial functions from a bipartisan group to one individual.[255]

Meanwhile, whereas Section 3 of Plan No. 2 had few defenders in the House debate, several more materialized before the Senate, possibly roused by House's resolve to block it. Frederick Lawton, Administrative Assistant to the Director of the Bureau of the Budget, spoke at length in defense of transferring the employees' compensation functions to the Federal Security Agency. He defused opposition from one camp by pointing out that the change would impact only the 37% of cases handled by the Commission which involved injuries of federal civilian employees (FECA claims). Most claims involved longshoremen and harbor workers, who were covered not by FECA but by a separate act, and whose cases were delegated by the Commission to regionally distributed deputy commissioners. Those claimants enjoyed (and still enjoy) the right to appeal decisions made by deputy commissioners to federal district courts, and Mr. Lawton assured his audience that process would not change.[256]

Mr. Lawton maintained that abolishing the Employees' Compensation Commission and integrating its functions into the Federal Security Agency achieved two purposes that were authorized by the Reorganization Act of 1945: consolidating agencies and functions according to major purposes, and reducing the total number of agencies. However, when pressed by Senator Wiley, Mr. Lawton could not say whether Plan No. 2 might result in any savings for the Government.[257] This mattered because the Reorganization Act was clear about expecting plans created under its authority to save money: "It is the expectation of the Congress that the transfers, consolidations, coordinations, and abolitions under this Act shall accomplish an over-all reduction of at least 25 per centum in the administrative costs of the agency or agencies affected."[258]

Mr. Lawton insisted there was nothing worrisome or even novel about staffing an agency with a single administrator and a board of appeals freely chosen by him without regard to bipartisan balance. He claimed similar arrangements were successfully used by the Social Security Board and a few other agencies.[259] In reality, although the originally stand-alone Social Security Board had been absorbed by the Federal Security Agency in 1939, it had thus far been allowed to continue operating as an independent, bipartisan, three-person body much like the Employees' Compensation Commission.[260] What changed in 1939 was just that the Board took on additional responsibilities and its Chairman began reporting to the FSA Administrator rather than directly to the President; then in 1940, it delegated the hearing and deciding of appeals to 12 referees who were overseen by a new Office of Appeals Council. Ironically, Section 4 of Plan No. 2 of 1946 was about to hand the Social Security Board the same fate Section 3 would hand the Employees' Compensation Commission, abolishing the Board and giving its functions to the FSA Administrator.[261]

It's worth noting that the Social Security Administration's (SSA) status as an independent agency was restored in 1995, and it's now led by an administrator with a seven-member bipartisan advisory board. Board members serve six-year terms and are appointed by the President, Senate, and House of Representatives in accordance with rules that ensure bipartisan balance. The Spring 1995 Social Security Bulletin explained why:

> The impetus behind an independent SSA emanated primarily from a desire to separate Social Security policy-making from economic and budgetary decisions affecting the rest of the Federal Government. Considering Social Security unique among Federal social programs because of its self-financing nature and "implied compact" with the nation's workers to pay "earned" retirement, survivor, and disability benefits, proponents of SSA's independence wanted to insulate it from everyday political, fiscal, and operational policy decisions of the Government."[262]

Of course, a similar argument could be made for insulating workers' compensation programs, which also fulfill an implied compact with the nation's workers and which are under constant political duress to curtail spending by reducing benefits. Unlike Social

Security claimants, FECA claimants are barred from appealing benefit decision to federal courts, making them even more vulnerable
to austere policy changes.

The 1946 debates highlighted what a great boon reorganization
power was to presidents and to those who had influence over their
plans. In reference to Plans No. 1, 2, and 3 of 1946, their patron Harold Smith raved about the process:

> The plans represent a highly expeditious way of accom-
> plishing much-needed improvements in the structure
> and administration of the executive branch. Under nor-
> mal procedure, the 28 provisions contained in the plans
> would not be enacted except by that many separate
> statutes. The principles of legislative-executive team-
> work contained in the Reorganization Act make it pos-
> sible for all of the proposals to be considered in a single
> group of documents and for a decision to be taken upon
> them within a period of 60 days.[263]

Congress could not amend reorganization plans as it could bills;
even the widest-reaching plans had to be accepted as-is or not at
all, creating strong political pressure from constituents who clamored for specific provisions. The only way for Congress to prevent
one bad provision from being enacted was by drumming up
enough support to block the entire plan, popular provisions and all.
In reference to Section 3 of Plan No. 2 specifically, Clarence Stinson
told the Senate: "Now, I am convinced that if the compensation
plan was brought before this committee, or the committee of the
House by itself, that it would not have a chance of being enacted
into law. But it is cleverly tucked into this provision where there are
several good features, and as a result of that, we reluctantly are
compelled to appear before the committee and ask for the entire
rejection of plan 2."[264]

In attempting to make sense of a plan to abolish a commission
which by all accounts had been performing its duties efficiently and
economically for 30 years, George Riley concluded that it was the

product of a power grab. He had been assured by President Truman's administrative assistant Raymond Zimmerman that none of Truman's reorganization plans of 1946 would touch the Compensation Commission. When Plan No. 2 was released, Mr. Zimmerman seemed just as surprised as Mr. Riley to discover that the Commission had been engulfed by it.[265] Though the Bureau of the Budget oversaw the preparation of the plan, there were numerous individual contributors inside the Bureau and out who weren't publicly acknowledged.[266] One person known to have played a role was Mrs. Eugene Meyer, chairperson of the Women's Foundation of New York City, who was an ardent, outspoken, and idealistic proponent of a centralized education, health, and welfare program. Mr. Riley couldn't help but notice that Reorganization Plan No. 2 closely resembled a report previously published by Mrs. Meyer's Foundation, called "The Community Road to Reorganization."[267] Mrs. Meyer saw no value in independent agencies and believed a single administrator to be always more effective than a board. She told Congress, "I actually think that these Federal commissions which float in the air with no responsibility to anybody are not sound administratively."[268] Shortly after Plan No. 2 was created, Mrs. Meyers' husband Eugene gave a high salaried job to Harold Smith, whose position as Director of the Bureau of the Budget went to a man named Mr. Appleby who was also believed to have helped devise the plan.[269]

On the last day of Senate hearings, Mr. Lawton's talking points were reiterated by John W. Snyder, Secretary of the Treasury, and by Watson B. Miller, Administrator of the Federal Security Agency. Mr. Snyder appeared before the Senate at the request of the President, in part to refute Councilman Riley's insinuation that Plan No. 2 didn't really reflect Truman's ideas but rather those of Mrs. Eugene Meyer and the Women's Foundation of New York City. He also attempted to allay fears about all three of Truman's 1946 plans by assuring his audience: "There is no way, under the Reorganization Act, that the substantive provisions of legislation—as opposed to organizational provisions—can be changed. And these reorganization plans make no such changes."[270] Mr. Snyder and Mr. Miller each separately touched upon the same themes Mr. Lawton had, and Mr. Miller also contributed his observation that the Employees' Compensation Commission relied on cooperation from the Public Health Service and Office of Vocational Rehabilitation, both of which were already part of the FSA[271] — so even if there were no overlapping or duplicated functions in the FSA to help justify absorbing the Commission, the FSA had at least some *related* functions, not all of which pertained to welfare.

The harshest blow to the case against Section 3 of Plan No. 2 came in the form of a memo from Acting Solicitor General George T. Washington, in which he contested the allegation that abolishing the bipartisan Employees' Compensation Commission and giving its authority to the FSA Administrator would violate Paragraph 5(a)(6) of the Reorganization Act of 1945 by imposing greater limitation on quasi-judicial functions. Mr. Washington outlined several counterpoints in his memo: (1) the FSA Administrator was subject to no greater outside controls, such as political partisanship or interference from another agency, than was the Employees' Compensation Commission; (2) Longshore and Harbor Workers would retain their right to appeal in federal courts; and (3) if anything, federal civilians would have access to a *more* independent review of their appeals under the FSA because the appeals board established by the FSA Administrator would be a separate entity from the bureau he established to make initial determinations.

Essentially, it was Mr. Washington's position that loss of independence in executing a function could not be presumed just because the function was transferred from a bipartisan commission to a single department head. His memo stated, in part:

> The full discretion now vested by law in one independent agency of the Government, the Compensation Commission, is transferred by section 3 of the plan to another independent agency of the Government, the Federal Security Agency ... It follows, therefore, that

under the provisions of the plan the Federal Security Agency may fulfill the functions transferred with no "greater limitation upon the exercise of independent judgment and discretion to the full extent authorized by law" than now exists in the case of the Compensation Commission.[272]

It was disingenuous of Mr. Washington to use the independent status of the Federal Security Agency as a prop for his position, given that President Truman's message transmitting the plan to Congress had announced his intention to "soon recommend to the Congress that legislation be promptly enacted making the FSA an executive department."[273] It worked just well enough, though—in a vote of 41 to 42, the Senate chose not to oppose Reorganization Plan No. 2.[274] With no concurrent resolution to block it, the plan took effect on July 15, 1946. FSA Administrator Watson Miller established the Bureau of Employees' Compensation under the supervision of a Director to whom he delegated most of the duties, powers, and functions of the U.S. Employees' Compensation Commission. He also established the Employees' Compensation Appeals Board, or ECAB, which was (and still is) a three-member quasi-judicial body which hears and makes final decisions on appeals. But the FSA turned out to be only a very temporary waypoint for FECA administration.

In 1947, Truman assembled a Commission on Organization of the Executive Branch of the Government—known as the Hoover Commission because it was chaired by former President Herbert Hoover—to study the matter and make recommendations. The Commission published its findings and recommendations in a series of 19 reports in 1949. Report No. 13 warned that the Department of Labor had "been steadily denuded of functions at one time established within it" and had been left with "about the same number of top officials as certain other departments with 100 times the expenditures and number of employees." It advised that the Department "should be given more essential work to do if it is to maintain a significance comparable to the other great executive departments." The Bureau of Workers' Compensation was suggested as a good fit because its "work in safety, statistics, and industrial standards is allied with other Department of Labor functions."[275]

In 1949, Truman's presidential reorganization authority was renewed. The Reorganization Act of 1949 did not exempt any agencies from reorganization and did not prohibit changes that might weaken the independence of agencies in carrying out quasi-judicial or quasi-legislative functions. This additional leeway was balanced to some extent by allowing veto of the President's plans by either chamber of Congress rather than requiring both to be aligned in opposition. The authority was valid for nearly four years instead of just the usual two, giving President Truman time to submit 41 plans to Congress, only eleven of which were disapproved.[276] Acting on the advice of the Hoover Commission, Truman's Reorganization Plan No. 19 of 1950 transferred the Bureau of Employees' Compensation and the ECAB from the Federal Security Agency to the Department of Labor.

In his message transmitting Plan No. 19 of 1950 to Congress, Truman announced that "the reorganization plan is a further step in achieving the general objective of the commission to strengthen the Department of Labor by bringing within it labor functions which over many years have been scattered throughout the Executive Branch."[277] In outlining the history of FECA administration, Truman left out any mention of the controversy that had surrounded disbanding the Employees' Compensation Commission in 1946, and he downplayed the fact that his new reorganization plan would transfer FECA administration from an independent agency (the Federal Security Agency) to an executive department (the Department of Labor) headed by a presidential appointee. In fact, while Truman acknowledged the independence of the original Commission, he referred to the FSA not as an "independent agency" but as "one of the major constituents of the Executive Branch":

From 1916 to 1946 administration of this system was vested in an independent Employees' Compensation Commission. Due to the greatly increased complexity of the Federal Government, it was imperative that the independent status of that Commission be eliminated and that it be placed within one of the major constituents of the Executive Branch. Therefore, in 1946, the Employees' Compensation Commission was abolished and its functions were transferred to the Federal Security Agency.

Without formal opposition from either the House or the Senate, Reorganization Plan No. 19 of 1950 went into effect on May 24, 1950. The Bureau of Employees' Compensation and the Employees' Compensation Appeals Board were both transferred to the Department of Labor, whereupon the ECAB kept its name but the Bureau became the Office of Workers' Compensation Programs, or OWCP, as we still know it today. The Secretary of Labor assumed authority to direct and control OWCP, as well as to appoint members of the ECAB and decide its rules and regulations. Since 1950, the recovery rights of federal employees who sustain injuries or diseases on their jobs have been subject to the interpretation and control of a single revolving-door political appointee, the Secretary of Labor.

"... It has always been recognized as a matter of principle that the administration of a workmen's-compensation law be vested in an independent administrative body free from political influences and from the dominating control of a political agency."[278]

-William Green, President of the American Federation of Labor, 1932
(and former member of the 1911-1914 Ohio Legislature that enacted
Ohio's original workers' compensation law)

CHAPTER 22

The Constitution

Workers' compensation in the United States deprives insured citizens of access to health care plans for which we might be paying a lot of money—just when we need them most—and contends that this is okay because we are now able to get *some* medical care paid for by our employers or their workers' comp insurers. How *much* medical care will they provide? Well, however much they think we need; or rather, however much they *admit* to thinking we need. As if it weren't bad enough that they get away with not committing to any guaranteed standard of treatment, workers' comp administrators also claim expansive rights to our medical histories and exemption from laws requiring protection of that information. How can it be constitutional to strip law-abiding citizens of something as invaluable as a competitive health care plan and replace it with a stingy, bureaucratic "back to work" plan? How can it be constitutional to condition access even to that inferior substitute on giving up the protection of medical privacy laws?

In principle at least, workers' compensation was declared constitutional by the U.S. Supreme Court on March 6, 1917 in its ruling on *New York Central Railroad Company v. White*.[279] Jacob White was a night watchman for the New York Central Railroad Company who was fatally injured at work on September 2, 1914. Jacob's wife filed a claim and was awarded compensation by New York's Workmen's Compensation Commission in accordance with state law. The railroad company appealed all the way to the U.S. Supreme Court, primarily on the basis that awarding compensation in accordance with a no-fault workmen's compensation plan deprived it of property without due process of law and denied to it the equal protection of the laws, in violation of the Fourteenth Amendment's mandate that "no state shall make or enforce any law which shall abridge the privileges or immunities of citizens of the United States; nor shall any state deprive any person of life, liberty, or property, without due process of law; nor deny to any person within its jurisdiction the equal protection of the laws."

In the Court's written opinion, Associate Justice Mahlon Pitney defended the setting aside of common law defenses where they no longer serve the public's best interest, if they can be replaced with something more suitable. He wrote that taking away legal defenses is not analogous to taking away property, because "no person has a vested interest in any rule of law entitling him to insist that it shall remain unchanged for his benefit." In other words, the Fourteenth Amendment protects only the *vested* interests of American citizens—the things they already have—while preserving the government's right to make, change, or abolish laws (such tort laws) that might allow one to gain, or cause another to lose, vested property. Ultimately, the Supreme Court upheld workers' compensation law as constitutional, writing:

> It is plain that, on grounds of natural justice, it is not unreasonable for the State, while relieving the employer from responsibility for damages measured by common-law standards and payable in cases where he or those for whose conduct he is answerable are found to be at fault, to require him to contribute a reasonable amount, and according to a reasonable and definite scale, by way of compensation for the loss of earning power incurred in the common enterprise, irrespective of the question of negligence, instead of leaving the entire loss to rest where it may chance to fall – that is, upon the injured employee or his dependents. Nor can it be deemed arbitrary and unreasonable, from the

standpoint of the employee's interest, to supplant a system under which he assumed the entire risk of injury in ordinary cases, and in others had a right to recover an amount more or less speculative upon proving facts of negligence that often were difficult to prove, and substitute a system under which in all ordinary cases of accidental injury he is sure of a definite and easily ascertained compensation, not being obliged to assume the entire loss in any case but in all cases assuming any loss beyond the prescribed scale.

The phrase used above by the Supreme Court to describe what the worker lost when workers' compensation law supplanted the tort system – "a system under which he assumed the entire risk of injury in ordinary cases, and in others had a right to recover an amount more or less speculative upon proving facts of negligence" — speaks only of being barred from pursuing a potentially lucrative lawsuit. It says nothing about losing access to private or public health insurance benefits, which didn't exist in any recognizable form back then. The constitutionality of workers' compensation in the U.S. rests in large part on the premise that it disturbs no vested interests. That premise continually escapes fresh challenge while critics focus instead on the slippery red herring of proving benefits "inadequate."

The question of adequacy is certainly worth studying and discussing, but it's too ambiguous to drive lasting and substantial change; right or wrong, it's impractical and politically infeasible for one state or federal program to provide adequate benefits unless all do, and nobody is going to go first. This is why numerous well-written, meticulously researched books and articles on the subject have changed nothing. This is why we're still treading the same water nearly half a century after the National Commission authoritatively pronounced benefits inadequate in 1972. There are plenty of reasons why the system *ought* to change, but only reasons why it *must* change can overcome the monstrous inertia of the present system and force the hand of Justice. The question begging to be asked today is whether workers' compensation benefits are a fair replacement for the vested insurance benefits lost by most people who get hurt at work; and the answer to that is a definite and demonstrable No.

Group health insurance was a rarity until World War II, when employers began using it to entice and retain employees in a depleted workforce constrained by federally imposed wage controls. In 1940, fewer than 10% of Americans had private health insurance coverage; by 1950, more than half did.[280] In 2018, 67.3% were covered by a private plan, and 91.5% were covered by a plan of some type, either private or public.[281] Assuming premiums are paid in full and eligibility criteria are still satisfied, a health insurer cannot deny an enrollee any treatment recommended by an in-network provider which conforms to its published policies. However, exceptions are generally carved out for work-related injuries and illnesses that would be covered by workers' compensation, regardless of whether or not those benefits are claimed. This is the insurance company's perfectly valid way of securing its own piece of the workers' comp pie; after all, why should it pay for medical treatment that is the employer's legal responsibility? The problem is, there are no minimum standards at all for workers' compensation medical benefits, let alone standards that would make it an equitable substitute for the coverage lost by a person with health insurance who happens to be at work when he or she gets hurt.

Returning to *New York Central Railroad Company v. White*, the Railroad Company's charge that workers' compensation violated the Fourteenth Amendment by denying it equal protection of the laws got little attention from the Supreme Court and was not pressed by the Railroad Company. Now, a century later, the equal protection clause demands attention for a purely contemporary reason: Workers' compensation claimants are disenfranchised from the HIPAA Privacy Law that guards the medical privacy of every other American citizen. The value of that protection is manifest in a society where potentially damaging or embarrassing information can be disclosed to millions at the touch of a button. Yet it is taken away from injured workers in order to more fully protect the interests of workers' comp administrators by maximizing their leverage to deny claims and requests for medical treatment. Not only does this violate the Fourteenth Amendment's guarantee of equal protection of the laws, but the consequent plundering of a claimant's private information violates the spirit and intent of America's oldest privacy law, the Fourth Amendment's "right of the people to be secure in their persons, houses, papers, and effects, against unreasonable searches and seizures."

Workers' compensation, as implemented today in the U.S., has two features that are unconstitutional. The first is its failure to guarantee a standard of medical care equivalent to the one provided by insurance policies most working Americans pay for or receive as an employee benefit—thus depriving them of a vested interest if they get hurt at work. The second is its requirement that applicants sign away their HIPAA privacy rights—thus depriving them of equal protection of the laws and subjecting them to unreasonable searches of their personal information. Those sacrifices represent a stealthy yet seismic shift in the workers' compensation trade-off. They were not part of the bargain.

"Injured workers are undeniably placed in a different position with the state than other citizens when they must sacrifice medical privacy to obtain compensation for their injuries. This is especially troubling in a country where medical privacy is a federal right."[282]

-Ani Satz, Professor of Law at Emory University

CHAPTER 23

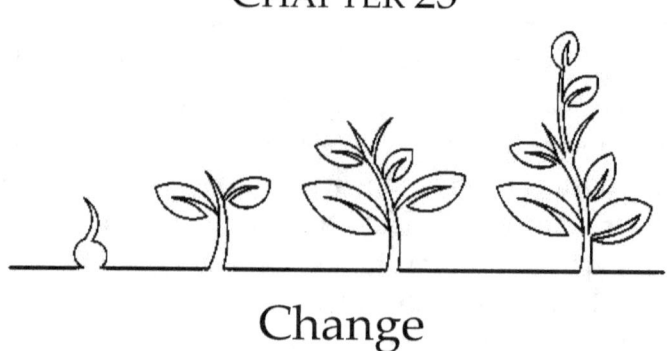

Change

The world is becoming safer for workers. The U.S. Bureau of Labor Statistics documented an industrial death rate of approximately 61 deaths per 100,000 workers in 1913.[283] It has since fallen to 3.5 per 100,000 workers.[284] This is welcome news, of course, and so is the great progress medical science has made in identifying causes and treatments for occupational diseases and wear and tear injuries such as carpal tunnel syndrome. Taken together, though, these trends blur the line between occupational and nonoccupational origins and weaken the causal relationship between safety practices and claims. The latent presentation of many occupational diseases means that diseases surfacing now may reflect past hazards that can no longer be controlled. There is a practical limit even to the extent to which *future* illnesses and injuries can be prevented. When every piece of manufacturing equipment has its guardrail installed and every walkway has been cleared of slipping or tripping hazards, and every area containing chemicals is well-ventilated, what more can an employer do?

The Federal Employees' Compensation Act of 1908 didn't pay for medical care, but the Act of 1916 did. As explained by the Employees' Compensation Commission in its 1918 Second Annual Report, "Under the Federal compensation act medical and hospital treatment is furnished without limit if application is made to the compensation commission, the only test being that it is reasonably required on account of the results of the injury."[285] The commissioners characterized medical care as a vital component of the benefits owed injured workers:

> The commission has felt keenly its responsibility in furnishing medical treatment. It has appreciated the solemn duty that rests upon it, not only to furnish medical treatment but to furnish the best available treatment, that which will be most certain to cause recovery from the injury and to restore useful function to injured parts. It feels the responsibility of furnishing that treatment which will most quickly and surely restore to usefulness the broken arms and the crushed legs, the perforated eyeballs and the fractured skulls, the fractured spines and the mashed hands.[286]

Unfortunately, in the early 1900s, there wasn't much even the best doctors could do for you, and medical practitioners not infrequently did more harm than good.[287] Narratives of cases processed by the Commission in its early years reveal a stage of medical science in which doctors couldn't be relied upon to do much more than set broken bones and suture wounds. They were of little help to patients with serious internal injuries and concussions. Take for example Arthur Schulz, a 27-year-old employee of the United States Experiment Farm in Mandan, North Dakota, who was pumping water on June 10, 1917, when the handle of the pump struck him in the head. According to the Commission's records[288]:

> He drove home himself in an automobile, a distance of 3 miles, and collapsed, being semiconscious for six hours. This condition cleared up, but he was dizzy and had headaches for four days thereafter. After June 17 he felt perfectly well until June 27, when he became depressed, and at 10 p.m. disappeared. He was later found at the country club sound asleep. After that time, up to July 5, his mind was alternately clear and hazy or confused.

Mr. Schulz's mother accompanied him to St. Paul, where he was seen by specialist Dr. H.O. Altnow. Dr. Altnow credibly diagnosed the problem as "an oedematous condition of the brain secondary to his cerebral concussion." Unfortunately, there was nothing he could do about it. On August 7, Mr. Schultz wandered away from home and was killed by a train. His death was accepted by the Commission as being work-related, based on the opinion of the Commission's medical officer that "Mr. Schulz would not have been in the way of the train had it not been for the melancholia, which was a sequel of the head injury."

Surgeons at the time were no match for traumatic internal injuries, and they may have tried to make up for it by over-diagnosing the two afflictions they best knew how to tackle: appendicitis and hernias, which appear with surprising regularity in the Commission's case files. In fact, the doctor who was called upon to treat a traumatic abdominal injury sustained by postal clerk Herman Mark in August 1917 was especially thorough, performing both a herniotomy and an appendectomy on him for a single charge of $75. In his report to the Commission, the doctor mentioned that he had performed a hernia operation on this same patient's other side 13 years prior.[289]

I took a personal interest the story of John Wardrop, a letter carrier in Pennsylvania who slipped and fell on icy pavement on February 20, 1917, landing on his back just as I would 100 years later. John kept working despite severe back pain until March 13, at which time he sought the help of Dr. Ford, who diagnosed him with a movable kidney. The Commission documented the course of treatment prescribed by Dr. Ford:

> Mr. Wardrop was put to bed, his side securely strapped, and a forced diet ordered. Dr. Ford stated that things were going along nicely, pain and other symptoms entirely gone, until unfortunately, on April 7, he developed an acute appendicitis, which abated in a few days only to return again on April 14, with a

slight rise in temperature. The physician then advised an operation, which was performed April 17. Dr. Ford stated that there is absolutely no question but that Mr. Wardrop's original trouble was entirely due to his kidney, and that the appendicitis was secondary, probably the result of inactivity and forced diet.

When hospital authorities examined Mr. Wardrop on the day before his appendectomy, they "found that his kidney had grown fast again," so the Commission fixed that as the point of time when he had healed from his work injury, and they approved wage compensation for him up to, but not after, the appendectomy.[290]

There were no antibiotics. Uncontrolled serious infection, known as blood poisoning, could arise from even minor injuries. Robert Hawkins was a driller in the Boston Navy Yard who was struck in the elbow by a flying piece of iron on March 27, 1918. No medical treatment was administered until three days later, when the wound was found to be infected. He died on April 21.[291] Disinfectants were available, but there was little consensus on their importance or appropriate use. Edward Kuehn was a machinist who accidentally punctured the ring finger of his left hand while operating a lathe on April 10, 1918. He tried to treat the wound himself at home by applying a pure solution of Lysol in the mistaken belief that it would speed healing. Instead, it burned his finger so badly that he was disabled for work and not awarded workers' compensation because his disability was blamed on the self-induced burn, not the original puncture wound.[292] Still, it's not hard to understand Mr. Kuehn's desperation to stave off infection. Another lathe operator, John McArdle, sustained a similar injury to his right index finger in October 1917, which also became infected and the finger had to be amputated.[293]

Some federal civilians worked and died in isolation, no help within reach. One of them was levee patrolman and gopher catcher Addison Ellison, who reportedly "met his death near Gadsden, Ariz., from an unknown cause, possibly, however, as the result of an attack upon him by an Indian on May 4, 1917."[294] Another was hunter and trapper Slate MacDonald, who died from an accidentally self-inflicted gunshot wound on October 5, 1917. The record states that "he realized the danger after the accident and wrote a note, tying it around his dog's neck, and sent the dog home for aid, but when they reached him, perhaps two hours afterwards, he was dead."[295]

Others had family or coworkers nearby, but lived too far from the nearest doctor to get timely treatment. When forest ranger Edward Wehrly developed a persistent, severe headache during an unusually taxing workday on December 29, 1916, he did his best to keep going, suffering without relief until the following morning, when he fell over dead while milking a cow. A doctor was notified immediately, but the Commission's narrative explains that "as no wagon road exists the entire distance between Basalt and Thomasville, Colo., and as no passenger or freight train on the Colorado Midland Railway was due for several hours, he was unable to come." Neighbors helped carry the body inside and checked it for signs of life: "The hands, feet, and face were cold, the body still warm. No pulse whatever or heartbeats could be detected. The mirror test showed the absence of respiration."[296]

In 1920, twelve years after passage of the first federal workers' compensation act and four years after passage of the second, the Band-Aid was invented. Penicillin was discovered in 1928 but wasn't put to practical use until 1941. The advance of medical science picked up momentum around then, with the first successful kidney transplant being performed in 1954, followed by the first heart transplant in 1967 and the first face transplant in 2005. Sophisticated medical care can be expensive. The average proportion of workers' comp benefits spent on medical care in the U.S. increased from one-third in 1985 to one-half in 2011. Once a 50-50 split was reached between medical and cash benefits, it stabilized there,[297] perhaps naturally or perhaps due to increasing reliance on medical treatment utilization review versus wage replacement limits to control costs.

Medical science has undergone a transformation, and so has the role played by workers' compensation administrators in brokering access to it. A century ago, effective health care was hard to come by. Medical technology and understanding were basic. Training and accreditation for physicians were inconsistent and generally weak.[298] Workers' comp administrators were challenged to find relatively capable physicians who were accessible to injured workers. In 1920, the U.S. Employees' Compensation Commissioners wrote that they had to give "particular attention to the medical supervision of cases of injured employees entitled to treatment under the act [in order] to protect the interests of the employees, many of whom would be in a large measure helpless to secure adequate and efficient treatment on their own initiative."[299] Today, most employed Americans have no trouble securing adequate and efficient treatment. Most of us have health insurance of some kind that affords us easy access to a plethora of credentialed providers we can sort by specialty, zip code, patient ratings, and so on.

In fact, medical treatment options have become so far-ranging that they must be rationed; decisions have to be made by someone regarding who gets which procedures and which medications. Availability of effective medical intervention is no longer the limiting factor; cost is. Workers' compensation administrators are no longer called upon to make treatment available to injured workers, but rather to guard the gate and make sure they don't get more than they definitely need. This is problematic because it's not in the administrator's best interest to pay for medical care that promises no commensurate gains in employability and productivity. Meanwhile, there are little savings to be squeezed out of formulaic benefits such as total wage replacement, and partial wage replacement can only be lowered so much by declaring disabled workers capable of earning more than they do. The wild card in the administrator's pocket is utilization review—controlling access to medical care. Medical benefits are just as expensive as cash benefits (and potentially even more so) but free from any hard and fast rules regarding how they must be meted out.

We wouldn't dream of trusting administrators to decide on a case-by-case basis how much wage replacement each disabled worker really "needs," and it's no less preposterous to let them decide how much medical care is needed. But who will manage an injured worker's medical care if not the workers' compensation administrator? Any reasonably competitive, defined level of care with a decent-sized network of providers would be a vast improvement over the tight-fisted utilization review guessing game injured workers are currently forced to play—assuming they can find a provider willing to play it along with them. The closest thing the U.S. has to a universal health care system is Medicare. It's not ideal, but it's a safety net that didn't exist when workers' compensation law was introduced to the United States, and it's a game changer. Not only would extending Medicare coverage to injured workers improve their lot, but it would obviate the need to shield Medicare from costs underhandedly shifted to it from workers' compensation programs that default on their obligations.

If we're going to do that, we might as well also expand Medicare's partner, the Social Security Disability Insurance program, to manage wage replacement for injured workers. This would once and for all rectify the gross inequity currently tolerated in benefits among states. The expansion of Social Security and Medicare to such an extent, while admittedly ambitious, is surely more efficient than maintaining 51 separately administered workers' compensation programs in the 50 states and the District of Columbia, plus the federal system. There will be no more easy way out for employers who currently underpay or pay nothing at all, and no more profits paid to insurers. As always, meaningful change will be resisted by those who are thriving off the problem: insurers, administrators, employers, doctors and lawyers who like things fine the way they are and don't care whether its right or wrong.

A popular, often-repeated fable about workers' compensation is that its high cost to employers motivates them to invest in workplace safety. Law professor and former West Virginia Workers' Compensation Commissioner Emily Spieler observed: "Nearly every monograph and treatise that has been written on workers' compensation has included what appears to be an obligatory chapter or section dedicated to prevention."[300] But Spieler's own experience and research led her to conclude that workers' compensation laws are not written with the intent of encouraging safety efforts, nor do they generally have that effect.[301] The "no fault" philosophy of workers' compensation, combined with an insufficiently clear link between the implementation of safety measures and the far-from-simple calculus of determining premium rates, can leave employers feeling victimized rather than empowered.[302] One thing we know for certain is that many employers are motivated to discourage injury reporting and fight claims, while the unequal relationship between employers and employees can make it risky for employees to fight back.

Before workers' compensation came along, the right to sue one's employer for negligence had value in and of itself, even when it wasn't exercised. In 1917, as a live witness to the rollout of workers' compensation laws in the U.S., Dr. I.M. Rubinow suggested that the new "exclusive remedy" might have taken away employers' most compelling reason to worry about accidents:

> The fact is that the despised "right to action," always present, had a market value of its own, because of the necessary cost of litigating the action in the courts and also because of the ever-present chance of a larger or smaller verdict. In consequence, only a very small proportion of cases ever reached the court, but in most cases where the injury was at all grave and the common law liability had been modified by statutory enactments, the claims were settled by the sale, as it were, of that right of action to the insurance company for some substantial consideration."[303]

In January 2018, an email went out to everyone working in my building from a person who, in addition to other full-time responsibilities, was filling in for our building manager, who had quit. The email warned us to be careful walking out to our cars because the parking lot was covered with sheet ice again, and it advised us that without a full-time building manager, we couldn't expect ice and snow removal this winter to be on par with services provided the previous winter. The previous winter was the one in which I had slipped on ice in that parking lot, breaking my back. It was no longer possible for me to imagine that my employing agency had any real concern for how its negligence had affected my life, or any aim to do better. I discovered that it's quick easy to file a complaint with OSHA. I can't say whether or not that made the difference, but the next time it snowed, there were people out shoveling every sidewalk leading up to my building, and there was even a salt truck in the parking lot. Let's see to it that OSHA has all the strength and support it needs to effectively promote, monitor and enforce workplace safety. After all, that's what it was actually designed to do.

If absolutely nothing else changes just yet, at the very least we need to stop letting insurers and administrators do all the talking about workers' compensation, adding insult to injury by molding public opinion in their favor with lies and distortions. Injured workers need a voice. I recommend requiring they all be given an opportunity to respond to an objective survey that records their experience and satisfaction. How easy or difficult was it to file a claim? How easy or difficult was it to obtain medical care? Were they treated with respect? Was their privacy protected? The results of that survey should be made public. Surely no one with nothing to hide would object to greater transparency and public awareness.

"The subject of workmen's compensation insurance has rarely been dramatized. It has no appeal for the average layman. It is usually when someone in the family, injured at work, is brought home in an ambulance or in a coffin that inquiry is made into workmen's compensation laws."[304]

-*Samuel Horovitz, Attorney and worker advocate, 1944*

References

[1] U.S. House of Representatives, *Compensation to Government Employees: Hearing Before the Committee on the Judiciary*, 60th Cong., 1st sess., 23 March 1908 (Washington: Government Printing Office, 1908), p. 20.

[2] U.S. House, *Compensation to Government Employees* (1908), p. 20.

[3] U.S. House, *Compensation to Government Employees* (1908), pp. 20-22.

[4] U.S. House, *Compensation to Government Employees* (1908), p. 23.

[5] Centers for Disease Control and Prevention, *Achievements in Public Health, 1900-1999: Improvements in Workplace Safety - United States* (1999), www.cdc.gov/mmwr/preview/mmwrhtml/mm4822a1.htm; U.S. Bureau of Labor Statistics, "Hours-based Fatal Injury Rates by Industry, Occupation, and Selected Demographic Characteristics, 2019," *Census of Fatal Occupational Injuries (CFOI)-Current and Revised Data*, https://www.bls.gov/iif/oshcfoi1.htm.

[6] U.S. House of Representatives, *Employers' Liability and Workmen's Compensation: Hearings on H.R. 20487 Before the Committee on the Judiciary*, 62nd Cong., 2nd sess., 15 March 1912 (Washington: Government Printing Office, 1913), p. 17.

[7] U.S. House, *Hearings on H.R. 20487* (1912), pp. 23-24.

[8] U S. House, *Hearings on H.R. 20487* (1912), pp. 23-25; Emily Spieler, "Perpetuating Risk? Workers' Compensation and the Persistence of Occupational Injuries," *Houston Law Review* Vol. 31, No. 1 (January 1994), pp. 163-164, http://hdl.handle.net/2047/d20002613.

[9] President Theodore Roosevelt, *Special Message of the President of the United States, Communicated to the Two Houses of Congress on January 31, 1908*, 60th Cong., 1st sess. (Washington: Government Printing Office, 1908), p. 2.

[10] *Ives v. South Buffalo Ry. Co.*, 201 N.Y. 271, 94 N.E. 431 (1911).

[11] *New York Central Ry. Co. v. White*, 243 U.S. 188 (1917); *Hawkins v. Bleakly*, 243 U.S. 210 (1917); *Mountain Timber Company, Plff. in Err., v. State of Washington*, 243 U.S. 219 (1917).

[12] David B. Torrey, "The Federalization/ Federal Standards Issue: A Short History Before and After NFIB v. Sebelius (U.S. 2012)," *Workers' Compensation Sections, American Bar Association 2013 Midwinter Seminar and Conference* (16 March 2013); Christopher Howard, "Workers' Compensation, Federalism, and the Heavy Hand of History," *Studies in American Political Development* Vol. 16 (Spring 2002), pp. 28-47, https://doi.org/10.1017/s0898588x02000020.

[13] U.S. House, *Compensation to Government Employees* (1908), p. 14.

[14] Griffin Murphy, Jay Patel, Elaine Weiss, and Leslie I. Boden, *Workers' Compensation: Benefits, Coverage, and Costs* (National Academy of Social Insurance: Washington, D.C., November 2020), pp. 48-49.

[15] National Academy of Social Insurance, *Benefits, Coverage, and Costs* (November 2020), p. 18.

[16] U.S. House of Representatives, *Federal Employees' Compensation, Serial 16, Part 1: Hearings on H.R. 15222 Before the Committee on the Judiciary*, 63rd Cong., 2nd sess., 31 March 1914 (Washington: Government Printing Office, 1914), p. 41.

[17] U.S. Department of Labor, *Injury Compensation for Federal Employees*, Publication CA-810 (2009 https://www.dol.gov/sites/dolgov/files/owcp/dfec/regs/compliance/DFECfolio/CA-810.pdf.

[18] U.S. House of Representatives Committee on Education and Labor, *Federal Employees' Compensation Act Amendments of 1960: Report to accompany H.R. 12383*, 86th Cong., 2nd sess., 2 June 1960, H. Report. No. 1743, pp. 3, 7.

[19] National Academy of Social Insurance, *Benefits, Coverage, and Costs* (November 2020) pp. 7-8, 24-25.

[20] "Bureau of workers' compensation – appointment, powers and duties of administrator – chief operating officer," *Ohio Revised Code* Sec. 4121.121 (2016).

[21] "Workers' compensation board of directors," *Ohio Revised Code* Sec. 4121.12 (2011).

[22] "Where an employer desires to secure the privilege to pay compensation and benefits directly," *Ohio Administrative Code* Sec. 4123-19-03 (2019).

23 Ohio Bureau of Workers' Compensation, *BWC Medical Guide*, https://www.bwc.ohio.gov/downloads/blankpdf/cd-106.pdf.

24 "Investment of surplus or reserve of state insurance fund," *Ohio Revised Code* Sec. 4123.44, (2007); "Disposition of insurance fund excess surplus," *Ohio Revised Code* Sec. 4123.321 (2007).

25 "Appellate procedure," *Ohio Administrative Code* Sec. 4123-3-18 (2019); "Notice of receipt of claim," *Ohio Revised Code* Sec. 4123.511 (2014); Ohio BWC, *Fact Sheet: Ohio Bureau of Workers' Compensation Claims Hearing Process* (June 2019), https://www.bwc.ohio.gov/downloads/blankpdf/hearpro.pdf; "District hearing officers – jurisdiction," *Ohio Revised Code* Sec. 4121.34 (1997); "Staff hearing officers – jurisdiction," *Ohio Revised Code* Sec. 4121.35 (1997); "Industrial commission," *Ohio Revised Code* Sec. 4121.02 (2014); "Appeal to court," *Ohio Revised Code* Sec. 4123.512 (2017); "Alternative dispute resolution for HPP medical issues," *Ohio Administrative Code* Sec. 4123-6-16 (2015).

26 "Workers' compensation ombudsperson system," *Ohio Revised Code* Sec. 4121.45 (2014); Ohio BWC Ombuds Office, *Ombuds Office 2016 Annual Report*, 17 April 2017, p. 4, https://www.ic.ohio.gov/service/ombudsreports-pdfs/ombuds2016report.pdf.

27 U.S. Bureau of Labor Statistics, *Employer Costs for Employee Compensation: Historical Listing*, pp. 2-9, 191-198, https://www.bls.gov/web/ecec/ecec-qrtn.pdf.

28 U.S. Department of Defense, *DoD Civilian Personnel Management System: Injury Compensation*, Instruction No. 1400.25-V810 (2005), pp. 7, 15, 24.

29 Insurance Information Institute, *Spotlight On: Workers Compensation*, 1 May 2017, p. 14, https://www.iii.org/article/spotlight-on-workers-compensation.

30 "May a claimant designate a representative?" 20 CFR 10.700; "Who may serve as a representative?" 20 CFR 10.701; "How are fees for services paid?" 20 CFR 10.702; "How are fee applications approved?" 20 CFR 10.703; "Representation; appearances and fees," 20 CFR 501.9.

31 U.S. House of Representatives, *Federal Employees' Compensation, Serial 16, Part 2: Hearings on H.R. 15222 Before the Committee on the Judiciary*, 63rd

Cong., 2nd sess. (Washington: Government Printing Office, 1914), 3 April 1914, p. 61.

[32] U.S. House, *Serial 16, Part 2: Hearings on H.R. 15222* (1914), pp. 61-62.

[33] "Adjustment after recovery from a third person," 5 U.S.C. 8132 (1974); "How much of any settlement or judgment must be paid to the United States?" 20 CFR 10.712.

[34] U.S. House, *Serial 16, Part 2: Hearings on H.R. 15222* (1914), p. 62.

[35] U.S. House, *Compensation to Government Employees* (1908), p. 45; Linda Darling-Hammond and Thomas J. Kniesner, *The Law and Economics of Workers' Compensation* (RAND Institute for Civil Justice, 1980), p. 32.

[36] "An Act to provide compensation for employees of the United States suffering injuries while in the performance of their duties, and for other purposes," Ch. 458, *U.S. Statutes at Large* Vol. 39 (1916), p. 742.

[37] 20 CFR 10.703.

[38] 20 CFR 501.9.

[39] U.S. Department of Labor, Employees' Compensation Appeals Board, *ECAB – Processing an Appeal*, https://www.dol.gov/agencies/ecab/resources/appeals.

[40] "Rules regarding fees," *Ohio Revised Code* Sec. 4123.06 (1995); "Fee controversies," *Ohio Administrative Code* Sec. 4123-3-24 (2009).

[41] "Appeal to court," *Ohio Revised Code* Sec. 4123.512 (2017).

[42] U.S. House of Representatives, *Amendment of Employees' Compensation Act: Hearing on H.R. 7960, H.R. 8530 and H.R. 8043 Before the Committee on the Judiciary*, 69th Cong., 1st sess., 2 February 1926 (Washington: Government Printing Office, 1926), p. 32.

[43] U.S. House of Representatives, *United States Employees' Compensation Act Amendments of 1949: Hearings on H.R. 3191 and Companion Bills Before a Special Subcommittee of the Committee on Education and Labor*, 81st Cong., 1st sess., 11-13 April and 2 May 1949 (Washington: Government Printing Office, 1949), p. 12; U.S. Senate, *United States Employees' Compensation Act Amendments: Hearings on S. 239, S. 800, S. 1245, and S. 1287 Before a Subcommittee of the Committee on Labor and Public Welfare*, 81st Cong., 1st

sess., 13-14 June 1949 (Washington: Government Printing Office, 1949), p. 47.

[44] U.S. House, *Compensation Act Amendments of 1949,* p. 21.

[45] "Federal Employees" Compensation Act Amendments of 1949," Ch. 691, *U.S. Statutes at Large* Vol. 63 (1949), p. 865.

[46] *U.S. Statutes at Large* Vol. 63 (1949), p. 865; U.S. House of Representatives, *Amendments to Federal Employees' Compensation Act*, Report No. 729, 81st Congress, 1st sess., 6 June 1949; U.S. Senate, *Amendments to Federal Employees' Compensation Act*, Report No. 836, 81st Congress, 1st sess., 4 August 1949.

[47] Amos T. Saunders, publ., *Proceedings of Conference of Commissions on Compensation for Industrial Accidents Held at Chicago, ILL., on November 10, 11, and 12, 1910* (Boston: Geo. H. Ellis Co., 1910), p. 119.

[48] *U.S. Statutes at Large* Vol. 63 (1949), p. 865; U.S. House, Report No. 729 (1949), p. 2.; U.S. Senate, Report No. 836 (1949), p. 10.

[49] *Castellanos v. Next Door Company, et al.*, No. SC13-2082 (2016); *Injured Workers Association of Utah, et al. v. State of Utah*, 2016 UT 20140372 (2016); *Nora Clower v. CVS Caremark Corporation*, 01-CV-2013-904687.00 (2017).

[50] U.S. Department of Labor, Office of Inspector General—Office of Audit, *Report to Office of Workers' Compensation Programs and Employees' Compensation Appeals Board: OWCP and ECAB Did Not Monitor the Representatives' Fees Process to Protect FECA Claimants from Excessive Fees*, Report. No. 03-16-001-04-431, 31 March 2016.

[51] U.S. DOL OIG, *Representatives' Fee Process*, p 10.

[52] U.S. Department of Labor, *Employees' Compensation Appeals Board*, Docket No. 16-1297, 9 May 2017, p. 3.

[53] Samuel B. Horovitz, *Injury and Death under Workmen's Compensation Laws (Horovitz on Workmen's Compensation)* (Boston: Wright & Potter Printing Co., 1944), p. 173.

[54] OWCP Provider Search Portal: https://owcpmed.dol.gov/portal/provider/search.

[55] Ohio Bureau of Workers' Compensation, *BWC Basics for Injured Workers*, https://www.bwc.ohio.gov/downloads/blankpdf/BWCBasicsInjured-Workers.pdf.

[56] Ohio BWC Provider Look-up Portal: https://www.bwc.ohio.gov/provider/services/providerlookup/nlbwc/ProviderSearch.aspx.

[57] Steven E. Levine and Ronald N. Kent, *Workers' Compensation Medical Fee Schedules: New Findings & Implications for California* (2007).

[58] Deloitte Consulting LLP, *Ohio Bureau of Workers' Compensation Comprehensive Study, Cost Controls: MCO Effectiveness* (25 March 2009), p. 6.

[59] U.S. Employees' Compensation Commission, *Second Annual Report, July 1, 1917, to June 30, 1918*, pp. 14-15.

[60] "Paperwork Reduction Act of 1995," Publ. L. 104-13, U.S. Statutes at Large Vol. 109 (1995), p. 163; 44 U.S.C. 3501 et seq. (1995); "Controlling Paperwork Burdens on the Public," 5 CFR 1320; John T. Spotila, *Estimating Paperwork Burden* (U.S. Office of Management and Budget, 4 October 1999), https://www.whitehouse.gov/wp-content/uploads/2017/11/Estimating-Paperwork-Burden-Oct14-1999.pdf.

[61] Levine and Kent, *Medical Fee Schedules*, p. 25.

[62] Barry Lipton, John Robertson, and Dan Corro, *Medicare and Workers Compensation Medical Cost Containment* (NCCI Holdings, Inc., 2010), p. 11; OWCP Fee Schedules: https://www.dol.gov/owcp/regs/feeschedule/accept.htm; Ohio BWC Fee Schedule Look-up Tool: https://www.bwc.ohio.gov/provider/services/feelookup/; Medicare Physician Fee Schedule Look-up Tool: https://www.cms.gov/apps/physician-fee-schedule/overview.aspx.

[63] DoDI 1400.25-V810, p. 65; "Common/Frequent FN Contacts," *Division of Federal Employees' Compensation Field Nurse Handbook* Part 3, Par. 4.

[64] "MCO scope of services—MCO medical management and claims management assistance," *Ohio Administrative Code* Sec. 4123-6-04.3 (2015); "Employee access to the HPP—employee choice of provider," *Ohio Administrative Code* Sec. 4123-6-06.2 (2015); "Where an employer desires to secure the privilege to pay compensation and benefits directly," *Ohio Administrative Code* Sec. 4123-19-03 (2019).

[65] U.S. Department of Labor, *Employees' Compensation Appeals Board*, Docket No. 16-1835, 4 May 2017.

[66] ECAB Docket No. 16-1835, p. 4.

[67] "Transfer or Termination of Authorization for Medical Care," *Division of Federal Employees' Compensation Procedure Manual* Chapter 3-0300, Par. 6.

[68] ECAB Docket No. 16-1835, p. 4.

[69] U.S. Department of Labor, *Employees' Compensation Appeals Board* Docket No. 90-1372, 28 November 1990, in *Digest and Decisions of the Employees' Compensation Appeals Board* Vol. 42, pp. 214-225.

[70] ECAB Docket No. 90-1372, *Digest and Decisions*, p. 220.

[71] ECAB Docket No. 90-1372, *Digest and Decisions*, p. 225.

[72] https://www.dol.gov/agencies/ecab/about/background.

[73] https://www.dol.gov/agencies/ecab/about/background.

[74] U.S. ECC, *Second Annual Report*, p. 175.

[75] National Academy of Social Insurance, *Benefits, Coverage, and Costs* (November 2020), pp. 5, 9-10, 68-69.

[76] National Academy of Social Insurance, *Benefits, Coverage, and Costs* (November 2020), pp. 94-99.

[77] "Total disability," 5 U.S.C. 8105 (1966); "Augmented compensation for dependents," 5 U.S.C. 8110 (1974); "Time of accrual of right," 5 U.S.C. 8117 (2006).

[78] National Academy of Social Insurance, *Benefits, Coverage, and Costs* (November 2020), pp. 36-38.

[79] "Total disability," 5 U.S.C. 8105; "What is total disability?" 20 CFR 10.400; "Compensation for permanent total disability," *Ohio Revised Code* Sec. 4123.58 (2006).

[80] "Permanent Total Disability," *Division of Federal Employees' Compensation Procedure Manual* Chapter 2-0808, Par. 3.

[81] National Academy of Social Insurance, *Benefits, Coverage, and Costs* (November 2020), pp. 94-99.

[82] National Academy of Social Insurance, *Benefits, Coverage, and Costs* (November 2020), pp. 36-38.

[83] U.S. House of Representatives, *Examining the Labor Department's Proposed Reforms to the FECA Program: Hearing Before the Subcommittee on Workforce Protections*, 113th Cong., 1st sess., 10 July 2013 (Washington: Government Printing Office, 2014), p. 66.

[84] "Compensation schedule," 5 U.S.C. 8107 (1974); "Partial disability compensation," *Ohio Revised Code* Sec. 4123.57 (2017).

[85] "Compensation schedule," 5 U.S.C. 8107 (1974); "Scheduled Disabilities," Ch. 691, *U.S. Statutes at Large* Vol. 63 (1949), p. 856; "Partial disability compensation," *Ohio Revised Code* Sec. 4123.57 (2017).

[86] "Funeral expenses; transportation of body," 5 U.S.C. 8134 (1966); Publ. L. 89-554, *U.S. Statutes at Large* Vol. 80 (1966), p. 548; "Making additional payments for medical or funeral expenses," *Ohio Revised Code* Sec. 4123.66 (2017).

[87] "Compensation in case of death," 5 U.S.C. 8133 (1990).

[88] "Benefits in case of death – dependency," *Ohio Revised Code* Sec. 4123.59 (1993).

[89] "Occupational Safety and Health Act of 1970," Publ. L. 91-596, Par. 27(d)(1), *U.S. Statutes at Large* Vol. 84 (1970), p. 1617.

[90] *The Report of The National Commission on State Workmen's Compensation Laws* (Washington: 1972), pp. 24-25, https://workerscompresources.com/?page_id=28.

[91] I.M. Rubinow, "Medical Benefits under Workmen's Compensation: I," *Journal of Political Economy* Vol. 25, No. 6 (June 1917), p. 582, https://www.jstor.org/stable/1819877.

[92] John F. Burton, Jr., "Should There Be a 21st Century National Commission on State Workers' Compensation Laws?" *IAIABC Journal* Vol. 51, No. 1 (2014).

[93] U.S. Department of Labor, *Does the Workers' Compensation System Fulfill its Obligations to Injured Workers?*, p. 2, https://www.dol.gov/sites/dolgov/files/OASP/files/WorkersCompensationSystemReport.pdf; Martha T.

McCluskey, "The Illusion of Efficiency in Workers' Compensation 'Reform,'" *Rutgers Law Review* Vol. 50, No. 3 (Spring 1998), pp. 704-715, 873-874; Amy Widman, *Workers' Compensation - A Cautionary Tale* (Center for Justice & Democracy, 2006), p. 2, https://www.centerjd.org/content/workers-compensation-cautionary-tale-national; Leslie I. Boden, Robert T. Reville, and Jeff Biddle, "Adequacy of Cash Benefits," *Workplace Injuries and Diseases: Prevention and Compensation: Essays in Honor of Terry Thomason* (Kalamazoo, MI: W.E. Upjohn Institute for Employment Research, 2005), pp. 37-39, https://doi.org/10.17848/9781429454919.ch3; Ted Rohrlich and Evelyn Larrubia, "Anti-Fraud Drive Proves Costly for Employees," *Los Angeles Times*, 7 August 2000.

[94] U.S. DOL, *Obligations to Injured Workers*, p. 13.

[95] Robert T. Reville et al., *An Evaluation of New Mexico Workers' Compensation Permanent Partial Disability and Return to Work* (RAND Institute for Civil Justice, 2001), p. 50; Boden, Reville, and Biddle, "Adequacy of Cash Benefits," p. 57.

[96] U.S. DOL, *Obligations to Injured Workers*; J. Paul Leigh and James P. Marcin, "Workers' Compensation Benefits and Shifting Costs for Occupational Injury and Illness," *Journal of Occupational and Environmental Medicine* Vol. 54, No. 4 (April 2012), pp. 445-450; David Michaels, *Adding Inequality to Injury: The Costs of Failing to Protect Workers on the Job* (U.S. Department of Labor, Occupational Safety and Health Administration, June 2015).

[97] Deloitte, *Ohio Bureau of Workers' Compensation Study*, p. 31.

[98] OWCP Medical Bill Processing Portal: https://owcpmed.dol.gov/.

[99] Patrice Woeppel, *Depraved Indifference: The Workers' Compensation System* (Bloomington, IN: iUniverse, 2008), p. 142.

[100] Woeppel, *Depraved Indifference*, p. 146.

[101] Ohio BWC Ombuds Office, *Ombuds Office 2015 Annual Report*, 19 October 2016, p. 8, https://www.ic.ohio.gov/service/ombudsreports-pdfs/ombuds2015report.pdf.

[102] Ohio BWC, *Fiscal Year 2018 Annual Report*, p. 29, https://www.ic.ohio.gov/news/annualreport_pdfs/bwc_ic_annual_2018.pdf.

[103] Ohio BWC, *Fiscal Year 2016 Report*, p. 27, https://www.ic.ohio.gov/news/annualreport_pdfs/bwc_ic_annual_2016.pdf.

[104] Ohio BWC, *Fiscal Year 2011 Report*, p. 5, https://www.ic.ohio.gov/news/annualreport_pdfs/bwc_ic_annual_2011.pdf.

[105] Ohio BWC, *Fiscal Year 2016 Report*, p. 32.

[106] Nedzad Arnautovic, *Workers Compensation and Prescription Drugs — 2018 Update*, (NCCI, 2019), pp. 11, 17.

[107] Arnautovic (NCCI), *Prescription Drugs*, p. 7.

[108] Ohio BWC, *Fiscal Year 2019 Annual Report*, p. 33, https://www.ic.ohio.gov/news/annualreport_pdfs/bwc_ic_annual_2019.pdf.

[109] Ohio BWC, *Fiscal Year 2019 Annual Report*, pp. 32-33.

[110] Ohio BWC, *Ombuds Office 2015 Annual Report*, p. 9.

[111] Ohio BWC Ombuds Office, *Ombuds Office 2014 Annual Report*, 21 April 2015, pp. 7-8, https://www.ic.ohio.gov/service/ombudsreports-pdfs/ombuds2014report.pdf.

[112] U.S. House, *Proposed Reforms to FECA*, 2013, p. 19.

[113] U.S. Government Accountability Office, *Federal Employees' Compensation Act: Analysis of Proposed Program Changes*, Report No. GAO-13-108, 26 October 2012.

[114] U.S. Department of Labor > OWCP > DFEC > *Enhancements to OWCP's Medical Authorization and Billing System*, https://www.dol.gov/owcp/dfec/regs/compliance/enhancements.htm.

[115] U.S. House of Representatives, *Second Deficiency Appropriation Bill, 1926: Hearing Before Subcommittee of House Committee on Appropriations*, 69th Congress, 1st sess. (Washington: Government Printing Office, 1926), pp. 1-17.

[116] Steve Andrews, "Lakeland Man Says Workers' Comp Denied Him Treatment After Explosion at Job," *WFLA Channel 8 News Station*, Tampa, FL (24 February 2019), https://www.wfla.com/8-on-your-side/investigations/lakeland-man-says-workers-comp-denied-him-treatment-after-explosion-at-job/; Steve Andrews, "Workers comp decides injured worker is fit for duty without tests," *WFLA Channel 8 News Station*, Tampa, FL (27

February 2019), https://www.wfla.com/8-on-your-side/investigations/workers-comp-decides-injured-worker-is-fit-for-duty-without-tests/.

[117] Mike Patten, "Who's Really Paying for Workers Comp?" *Leader's Edge*, 23 March 2016, https://www.leadersedge.com/industry/whos-really-paying-for-workers-comp.

[118] Darling-Hammond and Kniesner, *Law and Economics*, p. 22; McCluskey, "Illusion of Efficiency," p. 744; Spieler, "Perpetuating Risk?" p. 150; Willis J. Nordlund, "The Federal Employees' Compensation Act," *Monthly Labor Review* (September 1991), p. 11; Martin W. Elson and John F. Burton, Jr., "Workers' Compensation Insurance: Recent Trends in Employer Costs," *Monthly Labor Review*, March 1981.

[119] Saunders, *Conference of Commissions* (1910), pp. 99-100.

[120] Rubinow, "Medical Benefits," p. 607.

[121] U.S. House, *Hearing on H.R. 7960, H.R. 8530 and H.R. 8043*, p. 19.

[122] Rubinow, "Medical Benefits," p. 612.

[123] John B. Andrews, "Legal Protection for Workers in Unhealthful Trades," *American Labor Legislation Review* Vol. 2, Issue 2 (June 1912), pp. 356-362.

[124] U.S. House of Representatives, *Management Practices at the Office of Workers' Compensation Programs: Ninth Report by the Committee on Government Reform together with Additional Views*, House Report No. 106-1024 (Washington: U.S. Government Printing Office, 2000), p. 8.

[125] Eliyahu M. Goldratt and Jeff Cox, *The Goal: A Process of Ongoing Improvement*, 2nd ed., (Great Barrington, MA: North River Press, 1984).

[126] OWCP's Mission Statement: https://www.dol.gov/agencies/owcp/owcpmisvisgols.

[127] Ohio BWC's Vision/Mission Statement: https://info.bwc.ohio.gov/wps/portal/gov/bwc/about-bwc.

[128] Ohio BWC's MCO Report Card: https://www.bwc.ohio.gov/downloads/brochureware/brochures/reportcard.pdf.

[129] Deloitte, *Ohio Bureau of Workers' Compensation Study*, p. 23.

[130] 1-888OHIOCOMP's website: http://www.1-888-ohiocomp.com/.

[131] 3-hab's website: http://www.3hab.com/.

[132] Occupational Health Link's website: http://www.oehpmco.com/.

[133] "Concentra's Approach to Occupational Health," on Concentra's website: https://www.concentra.com/occupational-health/.

[134] Government Accountability Office, *Workplace Safety and Health: Enhancing OSHA's Records Audit Process Could Improve the Accuracy of Worker Injury and Illness Data*, Report No. GAO-10-10 (October 2009), p. 19; "General Recording Criteria," 29 CFR 1904.7.

[135] "Physical Therapy," *Division of Federal Employees' Compensation Procedure Manual* Chapter 2-0810, Par. 19.

[136] Ohio BWC, *Medical Guide*, p. 3.

[137] Ohio BWC, *Medical Guide*, p. 3.

[138] Ohio BWC, *Medical Guide*, p. 14.

[139] "Timeframes," *Division of Federal Employees' Compensation Field Nurse Handbook*, Part 3, Par. 7.

[140] Patten, "Who's Really Paying?"

[141] "The Genetic Information Nondiscrimination Act of 2008," Pub. L. 110-233 Sec. 209, Par. (a)(4), *U.S. Statutes at Large* Vol. 122, p. 919.

[142] Pub. L. 110-233 Sec. 2, Par. (5), *U.S. Statutes at Large* Vol. 122, p. 919.

[143] "Weighing Medical Evidence," *Division of Federal Employees' Compensation Procedure Manual* Chapter 2-0810, Par. 6.

[144] "Participants in the Nurse Intervention Program (NIP)," *Division of Federal Employees' Compensation Field Nurse Handbook* Part 2, Par. 3.

[145] "Authority," *Division of Federal Employees' Compensation Field Nurse Handbook* Part 2, Par. 1.

[146] Woeppel, *Depraved Indifference*, p. 150.

[147] Summary of the HIPAA Privacy Rule on the U.S. Department of Health & Human Services website: https://www.hhs.gov/hipaa/for-professionals/privacy/laws-regulations/index.html.

148 "Notice of privacy practices for protected health information," 45 CFR 164.520 (2013).

149 "The Health Insurance Portability and Accountability Act of 1996," Pub. L. 104-191, *U.S. Statutes at Large* Vol. 110 (1996), p. 1936.

150 "National Committee on Vital and Health Statistics: Publication of Recommendations Relating to HIPAA Health Data Standards; Notice," *Federal Register* Vol. 65, No. 132 (10 July 2000), p. 42371.

151 "Standards for Privacy of Individually Identifiable Health Information; Proposed Rule," *Federal Register* Vol. 64, No. 212 (3 November 1999), p. 59932.

152 64 F.R. 212 (3 November 1999), p. 59973.

153 Ani Satz, "The Federalism Challenges of Protecting Medical Privacy in Workers' Compensation," *Indiana Law Journal* Vol. 94, No. 4 (Fall 2019), pp. 1555-1611.

154 "Standards for Privacy of Individually Identifiable Health Information; Final Rule," *Federal Register* Vol. 65, No. 250 (28 December 2000), p. 82708.

155 65 F.R. 250 (28 December 2000), p. 82708.

156 65 F.R. 250 (28 December 2000), p. 82542.

157 Satz, "Protecting Medical Privacy," pp. 1583-1597.

158 The Department of Health and Human Services, *Disclosures for Workers' Compensation Purposes*: https://www.hhs.gov/hipaa/for-professionals/privacy/guidance/disclosures-workers-compensation/index.html.

159 64 F.R. 212 (3 November 1999), p. 60008.

160 HHS Answer to Frequently Asked Question: https://www.hhs.gov/hipaa/for-professionals/faq/327/am-i-permitted-to-disclose-information-regarding-an-injured-workers-previous-condition/index.html.

161 64 F.R. 212 (3 November 1999) p. 59940.

162 https://www.dol.gov/agencies/owcp/dcmwc/hipaa-notice. An identical notice was posted at https://www.dol.gov/owcp/contacts/dallas/HIPAA.htm, but was removed in February 2021.

[163] "Privacy Act of 1974: Publication in Full of All Notices of Systems of Records, Including Several New Systems, Substantive Amendments to Existing Systems, Decommissioning of Obsolete Legacy Systems, and Publication of Proposed Routine Uses," *Federal Register* Vol. 81, No. 83 (29 April 2016), p. 25777; Privacy Act Systems – DOL/GOVT-1: https://www.dol.gov/sol/privacy/dol-govt-1.htm.

[164] Privacy Act Systems – Universal Routine Uses of the Records: https://www.dol.gov/sol/privacy/intro.htm.

[165] Privacy Act Systems – DOL /GOVT-1: https://www.dol.gov/sol/privacy/dol-govt-1.htm.

[166] "Agency Requirements," 5 U.S.C. 552a, Par. (e).

[167] 81 F.R. 83 (29 April 2016), p. 25779.

[168] "How may a FECA claimant or beneficiary obtain copies of protected records?" 20 CFR 10.12.

[169] *Privacy Act – Personally Identifiable Information (PII)*, OWCP Bulletin No. 08-01, 23 January 2008, https://www.dol.gov/owcp/procedure-manual/OWCPBulletins/index.htm#OWCPB0801.

[170] "Criminal Penalties," 5 U.S.C. 552a, Par. (i).

[171] "Notification to Individuals," 45 CFR 164.404.

[172] "Wrongful disclosure of individually identifiable health information," 42 U.S.C. 1320d-6 (2009).

[173] Michael Kelley, *We're All Paying the Price of Employee-perpetuated Worker's Compensation Fraud* (Hub International, 29 September 2017): https://www.hubinternational.com/blog/2017/09/paying-the-price-of-workers-compensation-fraud/.

[174] David Corum, *Insurance Research Council Finds That Fraud and Buildup Add Up to $7.7 Billion in Excess Payments for Auto Injury Claims*, (IRC, 2015), https://www.insurance-research.org/sites/default/files/downloads/IRC%20Fraud%20News%20Release.pdf.

[175] J. Paul Leigh, Steven Markowitz, Marianne Fahs, and Philip Landrigan, *Costs of Occupational Injuries and Illnesses* (Ann Arbor: The University of Michigan Press), pp. 195-198; McCluskey, "Illusion of Efficiency," pp. 873-

893; Widman, *A Cautionary Tale*; GAO, *Enhancing OSHA's Records Audit Process*; Rohrlich and Larrubia, "Anti-Fraud Drive Proves Costly"; LexisNexis, "Employer Fraud in Workers' Compensation - Just How Significant is it?" (2008), https://www.lexisnexis.com/LegalNewsRoom/workers-compensation/b/workers-compensation-law-blog/posts/employer-fraud-in-workers 1920 -compensation- 1320 -just-how-significant-is-it 3f00 ; David Michaels, "Fraud in the Workers' Compensation System: Origin and Magnitude," *Occupational Medicine: State of the Art Reviews* Vol. 13, No. 2 (April-June 1998), pp. 439-442; Lisa Cullen, "The Myth of Workers' Compensation Fraud," *Frontline: A Dangerous Business* (9 January 2003), https://www.pbs.org/wgbh/pages/frontline/shows/workplace/etc/fraud.html; Greg Tarpinian, *Workers' Compensation Fraud: The Real Story* (Labor Research Association, June 1998), https://www.govinfo.gov/content/pkg/CREC-1998-10-11/html/CREC-1998-10-11-pt1-PgE2057.htm.

[176] Darling-Hammond and Kniesner, *Law and Economics*, p. 22; McCluskey, "Illusion of Efficiency," p. 744; Spieler, "Perpetuating Risk?" p. 150; Nordlund, "Federal Employees' Compensation Act," p. 11; Elson and Burton, "Recent Trends."

[177] Aaron C. Catlin and Cathy A. Cowan, *National Health Spending, 1960-2013* (Centers for Medicare & Medicaid Services: 2015), https://www.healthaffairs.org/do/10.1377/hblog20151123.051904/full/; George B. Moseley III, "The U.S. Health Care Non-System, 1908-2008,

AMA Journal of Ethics (May 2008), https://doi.org/10.1001/virtualmentor.2008.10.5.mhst1-0805.

[178] McCluskey, "Illusion of Efficiency," pp. 691-694; Widman, *A Cautionary Tale*; Spieler, "Perpetuating Risk?" pp. 152-154; Rohrlich and Larrubia, "Anti-Fraud Drive Proves Costly."

[179] Rohrlich and Larrubia, "Anti-Fraud Drive Proves Costly."

[180] Leigh et al., *Costs*, pp. 195-198; McCluskey, "Illusion of Efficiency," pp. 704-715, 873-893; Widman, *A Cautionary Tale*; Boden, Reville, and Biddle, "Adequacy of Cash Benefits," pp. 37-39; Rohrlich and Larrubia, "Anti-Fraud Drive Proves Costly"; LexisNexis, "Employer Fraud"; Michaels, "Origin and Magnitude," pp. 439-442; Cullen, "The Myth"; Tarpinian, *The Real Story*.

[181] Leigh et al., *Costs*, pp. 195-198; McCluskey, "Illusion of Efficiency," pp. 873-893; Widman, "A Cautionary Tale,"; LexisNexis, "Employer Fraud"; Michaels, "Origin and Magnitude," pp. 439-442; Cullen, "The Myth"; Tarpinian, *The Real Story*.

[182] McCluskey, "Illusion of Efficiency," pp. 875-876.

[183] U.S. House, *Proposed Reforms to FECA*, 2013.

[184] Mark Flatten, "Experts Say Fraud Rampant in Federal Worker Disability Program," *Washington Examiner*, 17 June 2013, https://www.washingtonexaminer.com/experts-say-fraud-rampant-in-federal-worker-disability-program.

[185] Editorial, "Congress Can't Afford to Ignore Civil Service Disability Fraud," *Washington Examiner*, 09 July 2013, https://www.washingtonexaminer.com/examiner-editorial-congress-cant-afford-to-ignore-civil-service-disability-fraud.

[186] Office of Inspector General for the U.S. Department of Labor, *Semiannual Report to Congress* Vol. 70 (April 1 - September 30, 2013), https://www.oig.dol.gov/semiannual.htm.

[187] Coalition Against Insurance Fraud, *An Analysis of Workers Compensation Outreach Materials to Combat Insurance Fraud*, April 1999.

[188] U.S. DOL, *Obligations to Injured Workers*; Michaels, *Adding Inequality to Injury*, pp. 6-7.

[189] Lauren Joe et al., "Using Multiple Data Sets for Public Health Tracking of Work-Related Injuries and Illnesses in California," *American Journal of Industrial Medicine* Vol. 57, No. 10 (2014), p. 9, https://doi.org/10.1002/ajim.22361.

[190] Letitia K. Davis et al., "Use of Multiple Data Sources for Surveillance of Work-Related Amputations in Massachusetts, Comparison with Official Estimates and Implications for National Surveillance," *American Journal of Industrial Medicine* Vol. 57, No. 10 (2014), p. 29, https://doi.org/10.1002/ajim.22327.

[191] U.S. DOL, *Obligations to Injured Workers*; Spieler, "Perpetuating Risk?" pp. 217-222; Emily Spieler and Gregory R. Wagner, "Counting Matters: Implications of Undercounting in the BLS Survey of Occupational Injuries

and Illnesses," *American Journal of Industrial Medicine* (October 2014), pp. 1078-1079, https://doi.org/10.1002/ajim.22382; Lenore S. Azaroff, Michael B. Lax, Charles Levenstein, and David H. Wegman, "Wounding the Messenger: The New Economy Makes Occupational Health Indicators Too Good to be True," *International Journal of Health Services* Vol. 34, No. 2 (2004), pp. 271-303, https://www.jstor.org/stable/45131335.

192 U.S. Bureau of Labor Statistics, "Nonfatal Occupational Injuries and Illnesses, 1976-2014," *TED: The Economics Daily* (29 April 2016), https://www.bls.gov/opub/ted/2016/nonfatal-occupational-injuries-and-illnesses-1976-2014.htm; U.S. BLS, "Employer-Reported Workplace Injuries and Illnesses—2017," 8 November 2018, https://www.bls.gov/news.release/archives/osh_11082018.pdf.

193 U.S. Bureau of Labor Statistics, "Census of Fatal Occupational Injuries, 1992," https://www.bls.gov/iif/oshwc/cfoi/cfoi_rates_1992.pdf; U.S. Bureau of Labor Statistics, "Hours-based Fatal Injury Rates by Industry, Occupation, and Selected Demographic Characteristics, 2017," *Census of Fatal Occupational Injuries (CFOI)-Current and Revised Data*, https://www.bls.gov/iif/oshcfoi1.htm#other; DHHS (NIOSH), *Worker Health Chartbook, 2000: Fatal Injury* (May 2002), p. 13, https://www.cdc.gov/niosh/docs/2000-127/pdfs/2000-127.pdf?id=10.26616/NIOSHPUB2000127.

194 Lee S. Friedman and Linda Forst, "The Impact of OSHA Recordkeeping Regulation Changes on Occupational Injury and Illness Trends in the U.S.: A Time-series Analysis," *Occupational Environmental Medicine* Vol. 64, No. 7 (2007), pp. 454-460, https://www.ncbi.nlm.nih.gov/pmc/articles/PMC2078472/.

195 GAO, *Enhancing OSHA's Records Audit Process*; Spieler and Wagner, "Counting Matters"; Azaroff et al., Wounding the Messenger," pp. 271-303; U.S. House of Representatives, *Hidden Tragedy: Underreporting of Workplace Injuries and Illnesses: A Majority Staff Report by the Committee on Education and Labor* (June 2008), pp. 19-21.

196 Azaroff et al., "Wounding the Messenger," p. 293.

197 Social Security Administration, "Table 9.B1—Coverage, benefits, and costs, selected years 1940-2011" in *Annual Statistical Supplement to the Social*

Security Bulletin, 2017, https://www.ssa.gov/policy/docs/statcomps/supplement/2017/supplement17.pdf; National Academy of Social Insurance, *Benefits, Coverage, and Costs* (November 2020), p. 46.

[198] Tarpinian, *The Real Story.*

[199] Pub. L. 89-554, Sec. 1919-1922, *U.S. Statutes at Large* Vol. 80 (1966), pp. 609-610.

[200] Pub. L. 103-322, *U.S. Statutes at Large* Vol. 108 (1994), p. 2147.

[201] Pub. L. 103-333, *U.S. Statutes at Large* Vol. 108 (1994), p. 2547.

[202] Ohio BWC, *Special Investigations Department Fiscal Year 2019 Annual Report*, p. 3.

[203] Ohio BWC, *SID Fiscal Year 2019 Annual Report*, p. 5.

[204] Ohio BWC, *Fiscal Year 2019 Annual Report*, p. 11.

[205] Ohio BWC, *Fiscal Year 2019 Annual Report*, p. 3.

[206] Bureau of Workers' Compensation Special Investigations Department Blog, May 2019, https://ohiobwcfraud.wordpress.com/2019/05/.

[207] Ohio BWC Special Investigations Department Blog, September 2019, https://ohiobwcfraud.wordpress.com/2019/09/.

[208] Ohio BWC Special Investigations Department Blog, July 2019, https://ohiobwcfraud.wordpress.com/2019/07/.

[209] Ohio BWC Special Investigations Department Blog, November 2018, https://ohiobwcfraud.wordpress.com/2018/11/.

[210] Ohio BWC Special Investigations Department Blog, November 2018, https://ohiobwcfraud.wordpress.com/2018/11/.

[211] Ohio BWC Special Investigations Department Blog, February 2019, https://ohiobwcfraud.wordpress.com/2019/02/.

[212] Ohio Bureau of Workers' Compensation, January 2019 press release: https://www.workcompwire.com/2019/01/ohio-bwc-recommends-largest-private-employer-rate-decrease-in-60-years/.

[213] Ohio Bureau of Workers' Compensation, June 2019 press release: https://www.nfib.com/content/nfib-in-my-state/economy/1-5-billion-rebate-by-ohio-bwc-welcome-news-to-employers/; July 2019 press release:

https://www.workcompwire.com/2019/07/ohio-bwc-board-approves-1-5-billion-dividend-for-ohio-employers/; September 2019 press release: https://www.workcompwire.com/2019/09/ohio-bwc-to-begin-mailing-up-to-1-5-billion-in-checks/.

214 "Bureau of workers' compensation – appointment, powers and duties of administrator – chief operating officer," *Ohio Revised Code* Sec. 4121.121 (2016).

215 Alan Pierce, *Workers' Compensation in the United States: The First 100 Years* (LexisNexis, 2011).

216 Horovitz, *Injury and Death,* p. 394.

217 Horovitz, *Injury and Death,* p. 386.

218 Amy Widman Widman, *A Cautionary Tale,* p. 3.

219 U.S. House, *Hearing on H.R. 7960, H.R. 8530 and H.R. 8043,* p. 17.

220 U.S. House, *Hearing on H.R. 7960, H.R. 8530 and H.R. 8043,* p. 18.

221 U.S. House of Representatives, *Amending United States Employees' Compensation Act: Hearing on H.R. 14226 Before the Committee on the Judiciary,* 67th Cong., 4th sess., 7 February 1923, p. 12 (Washington: Government Printing Office, 1923).

222 *McCann v. McCormack's Garage, Inc.,* 203 App. Div. 387.

223 State of New York Department of Labor, *Special Bulletin No. 123: Court Decisions on Workmen's Compensation Law; November, 1922-February, 1924,* 3 March 1924, p. 29.

224 Vickie Sandlin, "Mail Carrier Found Not Guilty on All Counts in OWCP Fraud Trial," *21st Century Postal Worker,* 27 July 2017, https://www.21cpw.com/mail-carrier-found-not-guilty-on-all-counts-in-owcp-fraud-trial/0.

225 "Forfeiture of benefits by convicted felons," 5 U.S.C. 8148 (1998).

226 LexisNexis, *When Do Misrepresentations by Injured Workers Cut Off Workers' Compensation Benefits?* (5 November 2009).

227 U.S. Office of Personnel Management, *Information About Disability Retirement (FERS),* https://www.opm.gov/forms/pdfimage/sf3112-2.pdf.

[228] U.S. ECC, *Second Annual Report*, p. 241; Gregory P. Guyton, "A Brief History of Workers' Compensation," *Iowa Orthopaedic Journal* Vol. 19, 1999, pp. 106-110; John S. Haller, Jr., "Industrial Accidents-Worker Compensation Laws and the Medical Response," *The Western Journal of Medicine*, Vol. 148 (March 1988), pp. 341-348.

[229] Horovitz, *Injury and Death*, p. 173.

[230] *U.S. Statutes at Large* Vol. 39 (1916), p. 742.

[231] U.S. House of Representatives, *To Amend the United States Employees' Compensation Act: Hearing on H.R. 7041 Before the Committee on the Judiciary*, 5 March 1924 (Washington: Government Printing Office, 1924), p. 8.

[232] "An Act To amend an Act entitled 'An Act to provide compensation for employees of the United States suffering injuries while in the performance of their duties, and for other purposes,' approved September 7, 1916," Ch. 261, *U.S Statutes at Large* Vol. 43 (1924), p. 389.

[233] U.S. House, *Hearing on H.R. 7041* (1924).

[234] U.S. House of Representatives, *Federal Employees' Compensation, Serial 16, Part 3: Hearings Before the Committee on the Judiciary*, 64th Cong., 1st sess., 28 January 1916 (Washington: Government Printing Office, 1916), pp. 30-32.

[235] U.S. House, *Hearing on H.R. 7041* (1924), pp. 5, 12; *U.S. Statutes at Large* Vol. 43 (1924), p. 389.

[236] "An Act To amend an Act entitled 'An Act to provide compensation for employees of the United States suffering injuries while in the performance of their duties, and for other purposes,' approved September 7, 1916, and Acts in amendment thereof," Ch. 695, *U.S. Statutes at Large* Vol. 44 (1926), p. 772; U.S. House, *Hearing on H.R. 7960, H.R. 8530 and H.R. 8043*.

[237] U.S. House, *Hearing on H.R. 7960, H.R. 8530 and H.R. 8043*, p. 11.

[238] Henry B. Hogue, *Presidential Reorganization Authority: History, Recent Initiatives, and Options for Congress* (Congressional Research Service, 11 December 2012), p. 6; "An Act making appropriations for the Legislative Branch of the Government for the fiscal year ending June 30, 1933, and for other purposes: Title IV-Reorganization of Executive Departments," Ch. 314, *U.S. Statutes at Large* Vol. 47 (1932), p. 413.

[239] Hogue, *Presidential Reorganization Authority*, pp. 8-9.

[240] "Reorganization Act of 1939," Ch. 36, *U.S. Statutes at Large* Vol. 53 (1939), p. 561; Hogue, *Presidential Reorganization Authority*, pp. 12-14.

[241] "Reorganization Plan No. 1 of 1939," *U.S. Code* Title 5, Appendix; President Franklin D. Roosevelt, *The President Presents Plan No. 1 to Carry Out the Provisions of the Reorganization Act: Message to Congress*, April 25, 1939.

[242] *U.S. Statutes at Large* Vol. 53 (1939), p. 561; Roosevelt, *Plan No. 1* (1939).

[243] Hogue, *Presidential Reorganization Authority*, pp. 13-14.

[244] "Reorganization Act of 1945," Ch. 582, *U.S. Statutes at Large* Vol. 59 (1945), p. 613.

[245] "Reorganization Plan No. 2 of 1946," *U.S. Code* Title 5, Appendix; President Harry S. Truman, *Special Message to the Congress Transmitting Reorganization Plan 2 of 1946*, 16 May 1946, https://www.trumanlibrary.gov/library/public-papers/117/special-message-congress-transmitting-reorganization-plan-2-1946.

[246] U.S. House of Representatives, *Reorganization Plans Nos. 1, 2, and 3 of 1946: Hearings on Concurrent Resolutions 151, 154, and 155, Before the Committee on Expenditures in the Executive Departments*, 79th Congress, 2nd sess., June 4, 5, 6, 7, 11, 12, and 13, 1946 (Washington: Government Printing Office, 1946).

[247] U.S. House, *Hearings on Resolutions 151, 154, and 155*, p. 333.

[248] U.S. House, *Hearings on Resolutions 151, 154, and 155*, p. 326.

[249] U.S. House, *Hearings on Resolutions 151, 154, and 155*, p. 203.

[250] U.S. House, *Hearings on Resolutions 151, 154, and 155*, p. 324; U.S. Senate, *President's Plan for Reorganization of Executive Departments: Hearings on Concurrent Resolutions 64, 65, and 66 Before the Committee on the Judiciary*, 79th Cong., 2nd sess., June 14, 15, 18, 20 21, 25, 26, and 27, 1946 (Washington: Government Printing Office, 1946), p. 468.

[251] U.S. House, *Hearings on Resolutions 151, 154, and 155*, pp. 206-207.

[252] U.S. House, *Hearings on Resolutions 151, 154, and 155*, p. 298.

253 Hogue, *Presidential Reorganization Authority*, p. 30; *INS v. Chadha*, 462 U.S. 919 (1983).

254 U.S. House of Representatives, *Reorganization Plan No. 2 of 1946*, Report No. 2327, 79th Congress, 2nd sess., 24 June 1946.

255 U.S. Senate, *Hearings on Resolutions 64, 65, and 66*.

256 U.S. Senate, *Hearings on Resolutions 64, 65, and 66*, p. 250.

257 U.S. Senate, *Hearings on Resolutions 64, 65, and 66*, pp. 255-256.

258 *U.S. Statutes at Large* Vol. 59 (1945), p. 613.

259 U.S. Senate, *Hearings on Resolutions 64, 65, and 66*, pp. 250-254.

260 Social Security Administration, Social Security History, https://www.ssa.gov/history/orghist.html.

261 U.S. Senate, *Hearings on Resolutions 64, 65, and 66*, pp. 334-335; Social Security Administration, *Hearings and Appeals: Brief History and Current Information about the Appeals Council*, https://www.ssa.gov/appeals/about_ac.html; "Reorganization Plan No. 1 of 1939," *U.S. Code* Title 5, Appendix; "Reorganization Plan No. 2 of 1946," *U.S. Code* Title 5, Appendix.

262 Social Security Administration, "Social Security Administration Created as an Independent Agency: Public Law 103-296" *Social Security Bulletin* Vol. 58, No. 1 (Spring 1995), https://www.ssa.gov/policy/docs/ssb/v58n1/v58n1p57.pdf.

263 U.S. House, *Hearings on Resolutions 151, 154, and 155*, p. 50.

264 U.S. Senate, *Hearings on Resolutions 64, 65, and 66*, p. 282.

265 U.S. Senate, *Hearings on Resolutions 64, 65, and 66*, pp. 166-169.

266 U.S. House, *Hearings on Resolutions 151, 154, and 155*, pp. 48, 93-94, 202; U.S. Senate, *Hearings on Resolutions 64, 65, and 66*, pp. 298-299.

267 U.S. House, *Hearings on Resolutions 151, 154, and 155*, pp. 164-167.

268 U.S. House, *Hearings on Resolutions 151, 154, and 155*, pp. 263, 278.

269 U.S. House, *Hearings on Resolutions 151, 154, and 155*, p. 293; U.S. Senate, *Hearings on Resolutions 64, 65, and 66*, p. 166.

270 U.S. Senate, *Hearings on Resolutions 64, 65, and 66*, p. 314.

271 U.S. Senate, *Hearings on Resolutions 64, 65, and 66*, pp. 328-329.

272 U.S. Senate, *Hearings on Resolutions 64, 65, and 66*, p. 429.

273 "Reorganization Plan No. 2 of 1946," *U.S. Code* Title 5, Appendix; Truman, *Transmitting Reorganization Plan 2 of 1946*.

274 U.S. House of Representatives—Vote on Concurrent Resolution 151 Against Reorganization Plan No. 2 (15 July 1946), https://voteview.com/rollcall/RS0790225.

275 U.S. Commission on Organization of the Executive Branch of the Government, *The Hoover Commission Report on Organization of the Executive Branch of the Government* (New York: McGraw-Hill, 1949), p. 327.

276 Hogue, *Presidential Reorganization Authority*, p. 21; "Reorganization Act of 1949," Ch. 226, *U.S. Statutes at Large* Vol. 63 (1949), p. 203.

277 President Harry S. Truman, *Special Message to the Congress Transmitting Reorganization Plan 19 of 1950*, 13 March 1950, https://www.trumanlibrary.gov/library/public-papers/74/special-message-congress-transmitting-reorganization-plan-19-1950.

278 U.S. House, *Hearings on Resolutions 151, 154, and 155*, p. 166.

279 *New York Central R. Co. v. White*, 243 U.S. 188 (1917), https://caselaw.findlaw.com/us-supreme-court/243/188.html.

280 Michael Morrisey, *Health Insurance*, 2nd ed. (Chicago: Health Administration Press, 2014), p. 12; Moseley, "U.S. Health Care Non-System."

281 Edward R. Berchick, Jessica C. Barnett, and Rachel D. Upton, *Health Insurance Coverage in the United States: 2018* (U.S. Census Bureau: November 2019), p.3, https://www.census.gov/library/publications/2019/demo/p60-267.html.

282 Satz, "Protecting Medical Privacy," p. 1610.

283 CDC, *1900-1999: Improvements in Workplace Safety* (1999).

284 U.S. Bureau of Labor Statistics, "Hours-based fatal injury rates by industry, occupation, and selected demographic characteristics, 2019," *Census of Fatal Occupational Injuries (CFOI)-Current and Revised Data*.

[285] U.S. Employees' Compensation Commission, *Sixth Annual Report: July 1, 1921 to June 30, 1922*, p. 53.

[286] U.S. ECC, *Second Annual Report*, p. 13.

[287] Moseley, "U.S. Health Care Non-System."

[288] U.S. ECC, *Second Annual Report*, pp. 70-71.

[289] U.S. ECC, *Second Annual Report*, pp. 149-151.

[290] U.S. ECC, *Second Annual Report*, pp. 90-91.

[291] U.S. ECC, *Second Annual Report*, p. 103.

[292] U.S. ECC, *Second Annual Report*, p. 121.

[293] U.S. ECC, *Second Annual Report*, pp. 231-232.

[294] U.S. ECC, *Second Annual Report*, pp. 74-75.

[295] U.S. ECC, *Second Annual Report*, pp. 82-83.

[296] U.S. ECC, *Second Annual Report*, pp. 140-144.

[297] National Academy of Social Insurance, *Benefits, Coverage, and Costs* (November 2020), p. 36.

[298] Moseley, "U.S. Health Care Non-System."

[299] U.S. Employees' Compensation Commission, *Fourth Annual Report: July 1, 1919 to June 30, 1920*, p. 12.

[300] Spieler, "Perpetuating Risk?" p. 175.

[301] Spieler, "Perpetuating Risk?" p. 123.

[302] Spieler, "Perpetuating Risk?" pp. 187-210.

[303] Rubinow, "Medical Benefits," p. 583.

[304] Horovitz, *Injury and Death*, p. 1.

www.ingramcontent.com/pod-product-compliance
Lightning Source LLC
Chambersburg PA
CBHW070541220526
45467CB00003B/1015